If I Can Write, You Can Write

If I Can Write,
You Can Write

by Charlie W. Shedd

Writer's
Digest
Books

Cincinnati, Ohio

If I Can Write, You Can Write

Published by Writer's Digest Books, 9933 Alliance Road, Cincinnati, Ohio 45242. First edition.

Library of Congress Cataloging in Publication Data
Shedd, Charlie W.
    If I can write, you can write.
    Includes index.
    1. Christian literature—Authorship. 2. Shedd, Charlie W. I. Title.
BR44.S53   1984   808'.0662   84-13058
ISBN 0-89879-115-4

Design by Charleen Catt-Lyon.

CONTENTS

The Big "If" and
1   Your Dreams

If!

Of all the little words in our language is there any more brutal than "if"?

"*If* I could." "*If* I would."

"*If* I had." "*If* I hadn't."

"*If* only."

Do you have a favorite "if" to go with your dreams as a writer? "If only I knew what subjects would sell" . . . "If only I could meet the right people" . . . "If only the editors were smarter" . . . "If only I could have a little luck, only one small break."

Forever like the neon lights come our flashing ifs. Yet down this road there are no royalty checks. I should know. Like every successful writer on my list of friends, I've spent too much time "iffing."

Why then begin a book on writing with a nonproductive word?

Reason: There is one *if* all-important to success as a writer. The first word in this book's title is no accident. "If I can write, you can write" might mean many things; but the giant IF is this brutal fact:

You can write *IF* you will pay the price.

The price? *Hard, hard work!*

For long-term success as a writer there is no other way. No good fairy. No lucky number on a bingo card. No alternative.

DISCIPLINE

I do not know everything there is to know about writing. But what I do know, I know well. And one thing I know well is that successful writing is a horrendous discipline. It is long hours at the anvil with the hammer. Heating. Pounding. Shaping. Smoothing. Sharpening. Then doing it again, and again, and again. For forty years I've been heating, pounding, shaping, smoothing, sharpening. Still learning, still struggling, still wishing I knew some easier way, but I don't.

Like a constant metronome, throughout this book you'll hear—

4

Writing is a discipline.

Yet I promise you, one day the discipline will become part of the fun. Before we're through, I'll tell you some ways you can make that happen for you.

Then I will tell you my secrets for handling the days when the fun is gone. What can you do with the blue blue blues of rejection? I will also tell you how you can stand erect in the shower of stones. Criticism, negative reaction, how can you handle these? I know, and I'll tell you.

I will tell you my rules for writing. I'll give you a look at some tools I invented for word gathering, word usage.

I will tell you too what I know about editors and publishers; how they measure you; what it takes to get that exciting letter, "Enclosed please find contract."

Everything I know I will tell you for your success.

At this point I hear loud and clear, "Who is this character telling me I can write if he can write? Would he be surprised if he knew I'd never heard of him?"

No, he wouldn't be surprised, and he wouldn't be unhappy either. When some of your books have sold in the millions; when all your books sell and sell; when invitation after invitation comes for you to speak, to conduct a seminar, or to appear on a television show; when all of these exciting things happen, you'll be more than glad that some people never heard of you.

Yet you will also be glad for another thing. You'll be glad that someone, known or unknown, said, "I will help you realize your dreams." That's what I'd like to do for you.

SUCCESS

What is success?

Success probably has as many definitions as those trying to define it. Yet isn't there some common denominator here for the serious writer? I think there is, and to get at it, I ask you another question:

Why do you want to write? Is it to make money? Nothing the matter with that. Money is a positive if we know what to do with it.

Would you like to write to help people? Fine! All God's children got troubles these days, and heaven knows the whole world needs a lift.

Or would you like to write simply to express yourself? That's good too.

Good reasons every one, but what are *your* reasons?

Assignment 1: Write three sentences on "My Reasons for Wanting to Write."

_____

_____

_____

_____

_____

_____

_____

_____

Take thirty more lines if you need them. Then when you have finished your reasons, here is **Assignment 2:**

Write three more sentences (or thirty) on "My Definition of Success."

_____

_____

_____

_____

6

_____

_____

_____

_____

_____

_____

I think it only fair for you to know my definition of success. Had you asked me those two questions, I would want to know where you're coming from. So this is where I'm coming from:

Success for me is many things.
Success is money.
Success is fame.
Success is the thrill of expression.
Success is exuberance.
Success is one day reaching that high
terrain where the hard work and the joy
begin to blend.

Yet genuine success for me is something bigger than any of these.

I am a believer. I believe that I am no accident going somewhere to happen. I also believe that you aren't. I believe that I am unique, and you are. You are special, and I am.

We are divinely wrought with a Holy uniqueness, created for Holy purpose.

That being true
We tune in Upward
We listen
We learn
We share
We offer all our dreams
dedicate all our talents
that we may become channels for
The Divine Author.

7

Now let's go back to you.

DREAMS

Assignment 3: On these lines write your writing dreams. Describe where you'd like to be five years from now. Ten years. Twenty years. At the top of your mountain what do you see?

_____

_____

_____

_____

_____

_____

2 Your First Three Paragraphs

How can I help you?

I'd like to be clever here, to write my very best. All of us writing books for writers should write at our very best. So I would like to write with super touch, super wording, super phrasing. But that's not what you need from me. What you need from me is help.

How can I help?

I think I can help you most by asking you to write. Now. Before we go to Chapter 3, I want you to write three paragraphs.

On what?

On anything you'd like to write. And if you're not quite sure what you'd like to write, could you choose from one of these?

The Thing I Liked (Like) Most about My Home

The Person Who First Made Me Feel Loved

Why I Want to Write

The Race Question will Finally be Solved By _____

My Number One Problem Is _____

The Day I Became a Man/Woman

Perhaps you like the more abstract topics. If that's true, try one of these:

Life on Planet "X"

The Church of the Future

The Year 2000

You know I cannot make you write three paragraphs. Neither can I keep you from turning the page and reading on. But I can tell you this: You will get more out of this book if you write those three paragraphs.

Why? Because the following chapters are designed for you to be your own critic. One thing I hope to teach you is how to analyze your own writing.

After you have written your first three paragraphs I will give you my six cardinal rules. Six simple rules, plain vanilla rules, rules for more salable writing. But even more than teaching you my rules, I am hoping for something else. I am hoping that my rules will lead you to create your own rules.

So now for understanding my rules and for eventually making your own, write three paragraphs.

They may very well be the three most important paragraphs in this book.

Paragraph 1. _____

_____

_____

_____

_____

_____

11

Paragraph 2. _____

_____

_____

_____

_____

_____

Paragraph 3. _____

_____

_____

_____

_____

_____

3

What Are You Burning With?

In the next chapter we will move to those rules I promised you. I will ask you to analyze your first three paragraphs carefully. But before we do that I want you to do one more thing for yourself. I want you to answer this question: "What am I burning with?"

When I began writing, like most of the hopefuls I know, my thinking was highly amateurish. "You want to write for a living, Charlie? So start writing."

I was a young minister in Nebraska. For some time I'd been bothered with a scratchy throat. Now the doctor told me I had a tumor on my larynx. He did indeed hope it wasn't serious, but what if it was? If it was, I might lose my voice.

"Down in the valley, the valley so low, bend your head over, hear the wind blow." That was one chilling wind, one low valley. Four years college, three years seminary, two years pastorate. What can a clergyman do without a voice?

Like most ministers, I had done considerable writing of themes, reports, theses, book reviews. I had even had some success authoring for woodworking journals. Manual training courses in high school had given me a real reverence for wood. For several years I had been building furniture and selling the plans to craft magazines. Idea: If I could write for woodworkers, couldn't I write for others?

Naturally, I took all this to my best friend. Fortunately, my best friend was, and still is, my wife. Her name is Martha, and like her namesake of the Gospels, she has some rare talents.

This Martha too is a queen of the culinary arts, but that's not all. She has a superb pipeline to superb wisdom. So we talked. And we talked. And we talked.

Then one day she asked me one of the most important questions I've ever been asked. It is, I think, one of the most important questions anyone could ever ask you.

Question for all aspiring writers, the Martha question.

WHAT ARE YOU BURNING WITH?

14

Phrase it any way you like. Throw it up against your sky. Keep it where you can see it. Make it a constant center of reference. Revise it, add to it, rethink it, but never forget it. Why? Because you will be a better writer if you write from a caring heart. When you write from a caring heart, the writing is not such hard work. You'll also write with greater clarity and be more helpful to your reader.

Or if you prefer, use one of these starters:

What is first among my concerns?

What do I care most about?

What's number one on my agenda?

4   The Six Cardinal Rules

Cardinal rule 1: Fifteen words per sentence!

Go back now to your three paragraphs. How many words do you average per sentence?

Why does it matter? It matters because today's markets demand an economy of words. Very important phrase here: "economy of words."

Exercise: For one week do a check in your television time. Deliberately count. How many words per sentence do you see and hear?

Then do a similar check of the ads you read. TV, yes. But also billboard, magazine, newspaper, anywhere, observe the ad maker's ads.

At the end of one week's observation the per-sentence average is _____.

I can hear you saying: "You don't mean I am supposed to take my patterns from these mindbenders? This is ridiculous. I don't like it."

Can you hear me saying: "Certainly you must like what you write. Increasingly you must like what you write." But comes now another all-important question: "Will the editor like what you write?"

And what does the editor like? The editor likes to sell. He likes material he can sell; he likes writers he can sell; he likes publishers who have hired him to sell. This is one hard fact of the editor's office. So that hard fact being one of life's harder facts for writers, here's another assignment:

Assignment 1: Rewrite your three paragraphs using no more than fifteen words per sentence.

Note: Do not try to change your thought. Hold to your theme. Say what you said before, but this time in shorter sentences—fifteen words, ten, five, three, maybe even one word.

When you've completed the assignment, read it again. Is it clearer now? More attractive to the eye? Would the average reader understand it better? Stay with it longer?

Paragraph 1._____

18

_____

_____

_____

_____

_____

Paragraph 2. _____

_____

_____

_____

_____

Paragraph 3. _____

_____

_____

_____

_____

_____

_____

Often-asked question: "Do you know my favorite author averages twenty-six words per sentence? I counted them. And I should average fifteen?"

Answer: Yes, you should until (a) you are as good as your favorite author, (b) your books are as much in demand as your favorite author's, (c) you know as well as your favorite author when to break the rules for effect, and how.

_____

Cardinal rule 2: Do not use the same word twice in one sentence.

Now back to your three paragraphs.

How many times did you repeat words in a single sentence? Do a check of the writers you read. You'll be surprised. Most professionals seldom repeat even the smallest words.

Another tough assignment:

Where you have repeated, delete one usage of that word and select a substitute.

Cardinal rule 3: One adjective at a time!

Check: Is there anyplace in your first three paragraphs where you used two adjectives in a row?

Sure mark of the amateur—piling up description.

So here is another productive discipline. Whenever I use two adjectives or more together, I will select one. I will keep the one which can best stand alone. Or I will discard all I've put together and go for something better.

Cardinal rule 4: Two commas per sentence.

Assignment 2: Count your per-sentence use of commas. Certainly there will be some sentences with no commas, and that's good. But are there any sentences in the three paragraphs with more than two commas?

On thinking this rule through you'll see the improvement it brings. It keeps you from saying more than one thing at a time.

But that's not all. Rule 4 also prevents the overuse of adjectives.

Cardinal rule 5: Write like you talk!

20

In those first three paragraphs how much of the "natural you" comes through?

The dictionaries define "natural" as "unaffected . . . relaxed . . . spontaneous . . . true to self."

Using those dictionary definitions, on a scale of zero to 100 (70 for passing) give yourself a grade for writing what comes naturally.

Fact for today's writer:

Formality is one sure sign of insecurity. One aid for applying this rule is contractions—

"Should we not?" to "Shouldn't we?"

"Do you not?" to "Don't you?"

Cardinal rule 6: Do not insult the reader with the obvious!

Favorite illustration: "The great, gray girder fell to the earth below."

The editor who gave me this classic says, "Where else could it fall? Sure, if it fell straight up, that might be news. But who cares? Then in addition to that flaw, look at those adjectives piling up. (Plus one more thing: When you use alliteration, stick with the soft sounds: *M, L, W.* Never the *K*'s, the *G*'s, the *T*'s!)

Thanks, editor friend, for the lesson. I must avoid the likes of:

"King Henry is dead. He breathes no more."

"They went to the Sierras, out West."

"It was raining. The sky was gray."

Addendum to the cardinal rules: Every rule is to be broken!

Example: "We were at work in the trench. The dawn was gray around us; gray was the sky above; gray the snow in the pale light of dawn; gray the rags in which my fellow prisoners were clad, and gray their faces."

Victor Frankl

What is the matter with writing like that, repeating like that? *Absolutely nothing.* That kind of writing is *absolutely brilliant.* I should do so well. And you should. *Absolutely!* Which is a very good way to conclude our thoughts on the six cardinal rules.

Say it one more time: Remember, do not forget, keep it in mind, repeat it again and again—

Every rule is to be broken! But before I break the rules, I must know what rules I'm breaking!

5   The Importance of Beginning Somewhere

A centipede was happy quite
Until a frog in fun, asked,
"Pray, which leg comes after
which?"
This raised his mind
to such a pitch
He lay distracted in the ditch
Wondering which way to run.

Most of us have been there with the centipede. We were doing quite well, thank you. Then somebody messed us up with one too many questions. Can that happen to a writer? It certainly can, and because it can, here's another assignment:

Expand your first three paragraphs to a full-length statement. Such as—

A breezy piece for your whole family
A fun thing for your friends
Something for your Christmas mailing
A column for your church newsletter or club bulletin
A letter to the editor or a feature article so interesting even the most jaded old pro would say, "This we make a feature!"

"No way," you say. "I am simply not ready to lay it all out there." If that's how you feel, I understand, because I've been there too. But you *must* begin somewhere, and I beseech you— expand those first three paragraphs into *something!*

If after testing your first effort against rules 1, 2, and 3 you plain can't stand it anymore, don't let that put you in the ditch.* I know exactly how you're feeling, because times too numerous to mention, I've felt like that, and I still do.* Often.

---

*In this chapter, and from here on, I am deliberately breaking rules on occasion. (Some I've marked; others I've left for you to discover.) Why have I broken these rules? Because I hope you will train yourself to say, "Oh, he's breaking a rule. Was he careless here or deliberate?" You decide. But wherever you find a broken rule, you write it over better.

So will you. Often. Even at the height of your success you'll think sometimes, "How could I be so awful?"

If that's the feeling you get from your first three paragraphs, wad them up in a tiny wad, throw them away and start over.

Now write three more and add three and then three more and on until you begin to feel, "This has possibilities! I like it."*

You get my idea, don't you? I don't want you ever to be so rule-bound you're even slightly paralyzed by

"What if I do it wrong?"

or

"How can I ever make it?"

or

"Excuse me while I have a breakdown."

So even if you don't know exactly what you're doing, write! Please do! Before you go on to chapter 6, you must take what you've learned up to this point and proceed to do your thing.* Don't let Charlie, or anyone else, put you in the ditch wondering which way to run.*

6

Six More Rules—
The "I-Wills"

Affirmation: a solemn declaration . . . oath . . . assertion . . . meaning "I will"

These next six rules are affirmations; pledges I made to myself. Early in my writing I made them for my own good.

If you're like I am, your promises to yourself can be a real winner.

Rule 7. I will use only grab-me-quick beginnings.

Since it takes but several seconds to flip the television switch—one second to shut a book—less than that to turn the page of a magazine or newspaper—plus almost zero time to shift the eye in any reading—I hereby make it my aim to launch what I say with great care.

By this rule, what grade do I deserve for the start of my three-paragraph piece? _____

And what grade does each paragraph deserve? _____

Rule 8. I will keep it moving.

I will skill myself with the verbs. Verbs provide energy. They propel the story. They pace. They transfer feeling. Good writing *feels*. Verbs give vigor. Verbs are where the action is. Write it again, say it again, and again, and again. I will skill myself with the verbs.

At this stage in my writing career my grade for verb usage is _____.

Rule 9. I will become an expert in transition.

The amateur jerks me along. Transitions are for taking my

reader from sentence to sentence, paragraph to paragraph, section to section. I must become a master builder of bridges.

With me transition seems to come naturally. Yes _____
No _____

For rule 9 I grade myself _____.

Rule 10. I will make the negatives positive (most of the time).

Today's reader wants to know "where it's at," not where it isn't. The Lord for whom I write was the all-time Master of affirmation. He changed all law from "Thou shalt not" to "This do and thou shalt live." To follow His lead may require some psychological overhaul in my interior. Am I too much among the doomsayers?

On a scale of zero for ultranegative to 100 for ultrapositive my rating is _____.

Rule 11. I will avoid professional jargon.

Such as the Protestant Latin of theology—"transcendence," "incarnation"—and the gobbledygook of many fields: "metastasis," "interface," "existential," "ecumenism," "paradigm," "rubricize," "staticize," "dichotomies."

For today's reader—for the sales I hope to make—I will decontaminate my vernacular of the vague! Jargon keeps my reader at arm's length. This I do not want. I want to draw my reader close.

My grade for rule 11 is _____.

Rule 12. I will say it differently.*

I will develop the art of writing in happy surprises. With words I will paint pictures and sing songs. By long self-training I will master the science of picturesque speech.

Here I deserve _____.

28

---

*(This rule is so important I have given an entire chapter to it. See Chapter 12.)

7   Reader Focus

I am one superb drawer of ponies. Why? Because when I was a little boy, I wanted a pony with all my heart. But I never got a pony, and that broke my heart. (Well, almost it broke my heart.) So what did I do? Out of my hurt I became my world's number-one drawer of ponies. And like so many hard things do, that turned into one fine thing for me. Whenever I was bored in school, at home, church, I escaped to my pony world.*

I tell you this because there is one walloping lesson here for all of us writers. One day when my first son was beginning to draw, I found him drawing a pony. Dear little guy, he didn't have a pony either. Not then. So there he sat drawing hard, erasing, starting over, revising, improving, until finally he asked, "Will you help me, Daddy?"

Yes, I do know enough about fathering to admire what he had done. But even though I knew better, I made a colossal mistake. Instead of *helping* him as per his request, I *drew* a pony for him. Believe me, this was an especially beautiful pony. Nicely spotted, conformation excellent, one of my very best.

Then came the lesson I've never forgotten. Holding my pony up, turning it this way and that, in plaintive voice he said, "But Daddy! I wanted a pony *I* drew!"

Isn't that the longing cry of every person in the world?

---

*On this page I am deliberately overusing one word. One shouldn't do that, should one? I am also overusing one three-word phrase. Find it? One shouldn't do that either.

It is. And being translated from ponies to potential book buyers, I call it "reader focus."

Authors see manuscripts beaucoup from amateurs. They are brought to us by mail. At workshops, conferences, seminars they're brought. They may even be brought to our door with an amateur opener like this:

"I know you must be busy and I won't take more than a minute or two, but . . . "

But what? But this, but that, but a zillion buts for starters. All of which really mean, "But why won't somebody buy my stuff?"

So why won't they? Is it because this stuff really is stuff? Why is it really stuff? There could be many reasons, but almost always this is one:

It's slanted in the wrong direction—From the opening sentence it beams back to the author.

Say it again! One more time! Play the record over! Never forget! *Publishers buy for sales to readers!*

Why do readers buy? Readers buy because they've made that all-important decision.

"This book may do something for me. I think it might solve a problem, meet my needs, expand my mind.
"Perhaps it will even entertain me, enlighten me, inspire me. Some way I am hopeful it will give me value for my money."

This is rationale number one behind that ever-so-important term "reader focus." And blessed is the author who never forgets it!

Assignment 1: Write your own definition of "reader focus."

_____

_____

_____

_____

Assignment 2: Back now to those first three paragraphs. How do they come across against these reader questions:

What will this writer do for me?

Solve a problem, meet a need, expand my mind?

Will I be entertained, enlightened, inspired?

And if I buy this book, will it make me a better person?

If my grade for "reader focus" doesn't deserve 90 or above, what must I do to change it?

_____

_____

_____

_____

Assignment 3: Back to rule 7. Write an opening sentence so reader-focused any potential buyer would be inclined to buy.

If you decide your opening sentence is already irresistible, hurry. Finish, wrap, rush to publisher!

_____

_____

_____

_____

8   The "Little Stinker" Rules

How many rules does it take to make a good writer?
To make the best, how many? How many will it take for you?

Nobody knows, and if anybody did, whatever the number,
it might well be wrong tomorrow. My list is constantly growing, and yours will. As you write, you learn your strong points
and your weaknesses. As you improve here, you will see need
for improvement there.

So ask it again, how many rules?

After forty years my own list is somewhere in the hundred
range. Some of these I call "little stinkers."

**Rule 13: Subsidiary rule on repetitions (see rule 2): The longer I
can go before repeating words, the better my writing sounds.**

Super rugged discipline: Aim not to use the same word
twice in succeeding sentences . . . not to use a slightly different
word twice in the same paragraph . . . not to use the same un-
common word twice in one chapter . . . not to use a very unusual
word twice in the same book.

**Rule 14. Subsidiary rule on beginnings (see rule 7): Withhold
the most important item long enough to build up anticipation.**

Don't give away the key word, the key idea too soon. At the
same time I am accomplishing this little stinker I must also do
the opposite. My reader must be told soon enough what it's
about. Neat trick. Tough challenge.

Rule 15. So far as possible, keep moving toward the main thought.

The pro is a skillful roamer—far enough to make it interesting, yet never losing the landmark.

Rule 16. Check for identical word beginnings and word endings in one sentence.

Here's an example of the not-so-good: "He was considering resigning."

The expert writer also avoids "similars": "Whenever he was exasperated he exaggerated."

Note: Exceptions done intentionally may add some interest. Exceptions done intentionally can make for rhythm and swing.

Rule 17. Avoid threadbare word combinations—two-worders, or three!

Examples are "there is" . . . "there was" . . . "it is" . . . "it was" . . . "due to" . . . "he said" (anybody said) . . . "they had" . . . "who is" . . . "which was" . . . "have got" . . . "one who" . . . "a little" . . . "and finally" . . . "so good" (so anything) . . . "you know" . . . "of course" . . . and of course a bunch of others; you know!

Additions:

_____

_____

_____

_____

_____

_____

Rule 18. Check prepositions with an eye for elimination.

These are the buggers—*of, for, about, to, unto, upon, in, into, with, by, before.*

Small secret: Prepositions at the end of sentences usually mean one thing—this could be written some better way.

In these three chapters on rules I've given you only a sampling. As I told you, I have more than one hundred rules—cardinal rules, minor rules, "little stinker" rules. Getting heavy, isn't it? Yes, and in the little stinker category my list seems almost interminable, even to me.

Example: One grouping of my picky-pickies is labeled "Avoids." Can you manage a few more?

AVOIDS

Avoid "now" as a sentence starter.

. . . "Now it came to pass in those days" . . . very good copy in those days. But these days "now" has been worn to a rag. For me overuse of the "now" starter is one more certain sign that I'm letting my standards down.

Avoid the sweeping generalities.

Example (from a well-known religious writer): "One of the most striking ways in which a human being is unique among creatures is that, while all creatures die, man alone *knows* that he dies."

How does he know? Many an animal lover would debate him long here. Why do dogs, cats, and other four-legged creatures often go away to die?

And two more examples of the sweeping generality:

"Everybody's doing it."

"They all think so."

Fact: The more religious we are, the more we're tempted to speak for God. Warning: Today's readers are sure to be turned off by pontifical statements.

Another beatitude: Blessed is he who does not speak glibly beyond his own capacity!

Avoid the use of foreign language.

Do I aim to impress the reader with my couth? The use of

foreign language is no way to do it. This is one of those games no
writer can win.

The Latin phrase without explanation will discourage the
reader who doesn't know Latin. Yet the use of Latin *with* explanation insults the reader who does know Latin.

And, unless I'm a botanist, I best let the botanists write for
botanists.

Avoid the mixing of metaphors.

Garish example:

"You know the author who wrote, 'If they don't stop
shearing the sheep that laid the golden egg, they are
going to pump it dry.' "

Browne, *Christian's Journalism for Today.*
(Dr. Browne did not author that. He is giving us a garish example.)

Avoid the worn-out adjectives.

"fabulous"   "beautiful"   "awful"   "weird"
and you add some:

_____   _____   _____   _____

_____   _____   _____

Avoid the overuse of slang.

Slang is like garlic. It adds spice, but too much is too much.

Avoid the "almost-but-not-quites."

I call these subtle sidesteppings of the subconsciously tim-
id in me.

Examples:
"nearly everybody"
"lots of"
"approximately 430" (No fooling, I saw this in a recently published book.)

Avoid stacking illustrations.

When I am using two stories in a row, I must ask myself
this question:

38

Should I select one and let it stand or discard both and go for something better?

Fair questions, often asked:
"Won't this writing by rules cramp my style?". . . "I like to feel free, to let it happen, to flow.". . . "Don't you ever feel inhibited by your rules? Is the final result worth it? Do you understand what I'm saying?"

Straight from writers' workshops, and do I understand. For forty years, at least one million times, I've asked myself these questions. Do the rules get in my way? Do they cramp my style? Do they inhibit me? The honest answer is "Yes, yes, and yes." 39

Then comes that even more important question, "Is the final result worth it?"

Let's flash back to those five words, "I like to feel free." So do I, and I especially like this kind of freedom: freedom to call any editor anywhere; any publishing house; freedom to ask, "Would you like to look at my next manuscript?" That is one very fine freedom—one great feeling—and so is their "We'd love to look at your next manuscript."

I am also free to decide, "Which one of these many speaking invitations should I accept next?" Will it be that church in Oregon? Perhaps the college in Iowa? Maybe the troops in Germany? Sorting all these things through—that's one fun freedom too.

Free to be heard. Free to go anywhere. Free to decide how the dollars should be spent. Great freedoms.

Question: Won't the rules inhibit the aspiring writer?

Answer: Yes, they certainly will.

So?
So what did that ancient thinker mean by this quaint word from the Book?
"It is good for me that I bear the yoke in my youth."

---

9   Hurry!

Always one mark of the amateur is *hurry!*

My phone rang on a recent evening, and it was long-distance. I like long-distance calls. A touch of mystery. Who will it be? This was a young lady. She was a housewife, an aspiring writer, with a serious case of the hurry-ups.

"I am calling you because I have read your books, and I simply adore every one of them," etc., etc. Which being interpreted means, "Charlie, you're in for a long evening."

But it's also heady stuff, and may we learn how to keep it in perspective. She simply *adored* every one of my books. (She's doing better than I am.) But as the sound of her adoration died, I got the message. She hadn't called long-distance only to adore. What the lady wanted was sales. Right now.

"I have this huge emergency, see?" (Huge debt, huge bills, huge bill collectors, huge rush.) "It must be simply divine to sell like you sell." (It is.) "But what I want to know is how to do that, fast!"

You think I'm putting you on? You wait. Very funny! And pathetic! But I hope you'll never forget it. Back of those phone calls from aspiring writers is the buried question "How can I hurry the money?"

Now comes the dull thud. You can't!

If I can write, you can write. That's the good news. But always with the good news, some bad news. And the bad news is—there is no way to be a successful writer fast!

10   Reread! Rewrite! Rephrase! Redo!

Again and again and again and again and over and over and over and over, and over again and again. I have no statistics to prove it, but I am absolutely sure this is true—the success of any writer is in direct ratio to the number of times that writer goes back to write.

All the good writers I know are like this: They are seldom satisfied with their first efforts. And here we have one of the author's bloodiest disciplines.

To part with something I struggled to produce; to drop what I once thought excellent; to say good-bye to my own hard-earned words; all agony! But that's how it is. The better the writer, the sharper the knife!

Warning: Some things don't need revision. Since that is true, here is a subrule to the redo rule.

Subrule: Wait twenty-four hours and reread! Then wait seven days and do it again! In this time gap:

Weak transitions show up.
So do impotent verbs.
Drag is more apparent.
Rhythm can be improved.
Colorless adjectives are visible.
The whole thing is easier to picture from the reader's
    view.

Observation: Reading aloud is another big aid as I reread, rewrite, rephrase, redo. When I "hear" my writing, I "see" some things I hadn't seen before. Reading aloud to an honest critic is even better. Hearing an analysis of my words from another voice adds one more dimension to the total picture.

The Stork is Dead was first published fourteen years ago. It was and still is one of my most popular books. In 1984, *The Stork*, as it is affectionately known at the publisher's, was republished in a new edition.*

44 Written for junior high, high schoolers, and the college set, *The Stork* had an interesting start. After release of *Letters to Karen* and *Letters to Philip*, I had many invitations. (Together those two "letter" books have sold more than three million. As nearly as I can determine, this is what the publishers mean by that term "affectionately known.")

Anyway after the two "letters" books, one of my most exciting invitations came from *Teen Magazine*. Published in Hollywood, this monthly slick aims for the big markets, big sales. They invited me to write their "Sex and Dating" feature. I was to write my column, readers would respond, and then we'd see what happened.

What happened was thousands and thousands of letters. How many thousand? Together we estimated 25,000. Every possible theme, every possible question, every hope, every trauma.

Finally, bringing the whole thing into focus, I decided to summarize these findings in *The Stork is Dead*. As a book these things could reach more of the young, do more good, last longer. So the book sold and sold and sold itself straight into a new edition.

There are many good books on sex and dating. But how can we entice the young to even read them? One answer—put them

---

*The more frequently used term "second printing," "third printing," etc., is different from "second edition." Second editions are a special kind of thrill. What this means is that the publisher sees your offering now as a "bread and butter" book. The publisher makes this request because he sees the book as an ongoing best seller. Second editions do call for considerable rewriting, adding to, taking away, updating. But with all those extra royalties, who could fuss over such a nice request?

in letters. Psychologists say, "Any teenager has a subliminal desire to read any other teenager's mail."

So the book sold on. Why? According to the marketing experts, one reason for its sales was that built-in appeal—teen mail time!

But I know another reason why it sold and why it goes on selling. That reason: "Reread! Rewrite! Rephrase! Redo!"

One of the most popular chapters in *The Stork is Dead* is entitled "Kicks Have Kickbacks." How do I know it's popular? I know because I'm invited (more than I can go) to sit where the young sit and rap. And when we rap, "Kicks Have Kickbacks" will surface every time. 45

As an illustration of "reread, rewrite, rephrase, redo," you'll be interested in the evolution of "Kicks Have Kickbacks."

Originally the phrase read:

"In trying to line ourselves up for kicks, we may put
  ourselves in direct position for some kickbacks."

After weeks and days and many more revisions, it boiled down to, "When you are out for kicks, remember the kickbacks."

Then in the final edition (sixteen revisions later) this three-word title came through, "Kicks Have Kickbacks."

So the book sold and sold and sold, and it still sells and sells and sells. A witness to "reread, rewrite, rephrase, redo."

In order to get this four-word phrase through to me I started a collection years ago which I call "Economy of Words."

My "Economy of Words" collection is nothing more than sayings gathered from other authors. And this is how I use them.

I record each saying on a slip of paper and put it in my pocket notebook. "Pocket" as in double meaning. Pocket-size book in my pocket. But in addition, when I come on a pocket of time, I take out my pocket notebook. Here in these minutes I go over my slips and think. . . and think. . . and think. . . and I think until finally, whether I like it or not, the message comes through again: "Reread, rewrite, rephrase, redo."

From my slips on "Economy of Words" here are certain of my very favorites.

Any style I have insists on two
principles
    1. Use the fewest words possi-
ble
    2. Use the simplest words pos-
sible

Harry Dingman

46

When you can shorten a sen-
tence, do. The best sentence? The
shortest!

Gustave Flaubert

In composing, as a general rule,
run a pen through every other
word you've written. You have no
idea what vigor it will give your
style.

Sidney Smith

A pure style in writing results
from the rejection of everything
superfluous.

Anonymous

The written word
Should be clean as bone,
Clear as light,
Firm as stone.
Two words are not
As good as one.

Anonymous

---

*The fewer the words
that can be made
to convey an idea,
the clearer and the more
forceful the idea.*

          Lambuth

I also make notes to myself and for my pocket notebook. These too I carry until I believe what I myself have written.

47

*Truth: The more I reject my own
superfluous words, the less I will
be rejected at the publisher's.*

*Before the reader can hear me
flowing,
    There must be another
sound—snip, snip, snip, cut, cut,
cut . . .*

*If ever fourteen letters weighed a
ton, these are the fourteen letters: "Economy of Words."*

Technique for Difficult Farewells
Question: "I simply cannot bear to part with things I worked so hard on. Do you know what I mean?"

Answer: Yes, I know, and one thing I've done about that feeling is something you can do. Close at hand I keep what I call my "Gems for Later" file. In this I put the things I cut. (No, not everything, but everything I grieved to eliminate.) You can be sure it's a mammoth file, and how often do I go to it? Almost never. I wonder if this could be one reason. Putting some good things out of mind makes room for even better.

11

Monster in a Cave Door—
The Editor

Comes now the time for rummaging around in editors' heads. Here we face that oft-asked question, "Why does the editor take so long to give me an opinion?" (Change wording to your preference, but however it's phrased, the meaning comes clear, "Why would anyone half-smart fail utterly to recognize true quality?")

Have you heard this whimsical parable of the mighty dragon? High in his cave above the village he roared every day; sometimes all day. Morning, noon, and night he roared. And looking up, the fearful people saw him brooding, glowering, threatening. Small wonder even the bravest of the town fathers were afraid.

Finally, a certain small boy announced he would go against the dragon. With great maturity he said, "I will not live where fires cannot be lighted; where children do not play outside; where men stay away from the fields; and all in fear."

"I will go to face the dragon," said he. And though they tried to dissuade him, he went. Then making his way up the mountain, he saw a strange thing—the closer he came to the dragon's cave, the smaller the dragon seemed to be. At last when he arrived at the cave opening, a miracle—the mighty dragon had become a creature small enough to hold in one boy hand. Whereupon our hero took the tiny "monster-creature" and carried it back to his people.

This is a parable of editors and what will happen when you

get to know them. There was a time in my life when I thought of editors as awful dragons. Today, after thirty years and thirty books, I can assure you editors are exactly like the rest of us. Some are fat and some are thin. Some are friendly, some aren't. Some are vague and some are specific. Some will call you on the phone, some will hardly answer their mail. And they too are afraid.

Why are editors afraid? They're afraid of the boss, the management, the publisher; afraid of their own judgment; afraid of buying too many "dogs." ("Dogs" in editor nomenclature being books which cost but do not pay. Executive editors take a dim view of undereditors who cannot tell the difference between "dogs" and books which pay and pay and pay.)

Now to another thing about editors. All editors are busy. When you become a best seller, when they invite you for a visit, you'll see why. This is a sight you can hardly believe. That editor you've been trying to understand is not at all Mr. Cool, Ms. Neat and Prim. There under a stack of manuscripts, papers, notebooks, boxes—there behind that desk sits your monster. Look carefully now: Over here, buried in all this stuff, you'll see your own manuscript, maybe still unopened.

Or suppose it has been opened. Did you know it might have been referred to another editor? Some junior editor, latest addition to the staff, experience zero. Or good news, maybe your writing was so fine they've sent it to a group of readers for their evaluation. Or—oh beautiful, perhaps it's gone upstairs for final decision before the board.

Also did you know the editor probably won't even read every page you've written?

How do I know? I know because I stood one day in a publishing house and saw an editor read line one of a certain manuscript. Line one, no more, and then he put his rejection slip thereon, "return to sender."

Why would he read line one, no more? I asked him that, and this was his answer: "If I read this first sentence and I like it, I read right on to sentence two. If I like that, I head for sentence three, et cetera through paragraph one. Then I may turn to the last paragraph, I mean the last paragraph in the book—If I like that, I may get serious. This one I may buy."

You don't believe it! I wouldn't have believed it either if I hadn't seen it with my own eyes, heard it with my own ears.

So that *is* how it is, or something like it; and that is one reason why an answer from the editor seems to take forever.

Discouraging? Don't let it be. See it as a challenge. It's *your* challenge to make your material irresistible. You *can* do it. If I can, you can. You pay the price, and they'll pay you.

Are you still thinking the editor is a monster? Then I want you to know something else. Most of my editors are nice people, the kind you like to have in your home. They really are human, very human, like you and me. They're also hoping for the best for themselves and for their publisher. Take it from me, they're even hoping for the best for you, *especially if they think they can sell you.*

51

12

Tools:
Picturesque Speech

We flash back now to rule 12, page 28.

I will say it differently. I will develop the art of writing in happy surprises. With words I will paint pictures and sing songs. By long self-training I will master the science of picturesque speech.

Always this is one sure difference between ordinary writers and the steady best sellers. The steady best sellers say it with a fresh touch.

My picturesque speech collection is one of the most important tools I ever invented. My nickname for it is plain "P.S.," and you can believe this is no postscript. This is basic. "P.S." written in a book which I've been reading means, "I like this. Beautiful. Intriguing. Worth remembering." So I underline the statement as it stands and write P.S. beside it. From there it goes to my P.S. Notebooks. Plural, because I have two of these fat notebooks, two hundred pages each. Here are some sample sheets selected at random from my pages.

Only a fish can do the autobiog-
raphy of a fish.

Sandburg, Carl
The People, Yes

Wherever Paul went, they started
a revolution. Where I go, they
serve tea.

Anonymous

Grandma was a person who nev-
er entertained an unexpressed
thought.

Ellenwood, James Lee
Just and Durable Parents

A vast apparatus of superfluities.
Fenelon
Christian Perfection

The hour was early. Day and
night were still struggling in the
sky.

Asch, Sholem
The Nazarene

54

The waves of that experience,
five years later, are still breaking
on her shore.
Runbeck, Margaret
Time for Miss Boo

He commented on the speeches
of a certain American President
as leaving the impression of an
army of pompous phrases moving
over the landscape in search of
an idea.
Kennedy, Gerald
God's Good News

Scattered fragments, afloat on
the sea of inspiration.
Bounds, E. M.
Power Through Prayer

His mind was unhinged.
Morrison, Frank
Who Moved the Stone?

There are moments in a man's
life when he seems to be aware
of the delicate chiming of a bell.
Rittelmeyer, Friedrich
Rudolph Steiner Enters My Life

Note: All P.S. items are docketed for source. Marked "Anonymous," the meaning is, "Thank you, unknown friend. Whoever you are, wherever you are, I like your style."

Note: I make no effort to arrange my P.S. either alphabetically or by subject. Random placing suits me fine, and every few months (sometimes oftener) they give me a turn-on. I think you will sense how thumbing through all four hundred pages can be one high time. Appreciating, admiring, cogitating, ruminating, smiling, laughing, I saturate myself in this phantasmagoria of expression.

56

Question: Isn't this dangerous?

Answer: It could be. In most of us there is a touch of thievery. Some funny man says it for preachers:

> "He preaches best who stealeth best
> All things both great and small;
> For the great mind who preached them first,
> From nature stole them all."

Whimsical, sure, but also a sharp reminder. The word is "create," not "pilfer." Yet doesn't the wisdom writer tell it like it is—"There is no new thing under the sun"?

For me my P.S. tool works like this: These beautiful things in my collection, pondered over and over, sink into my subconscious. There they incubate, turn themselves, stimulate, develop. Then one day comes that fresh phrase I can honestly call my own.

Example: Ralph Gilbert was one of my minister friends. For years he pastored the First Presbyterian Church of Fremont, Nebraska. Usually when a man remains in one pulpit long, he's an above average preacher. Ralph was certainly that, and so much above average, I read his sermons every week. Every week he had them printed for his parish, and we made a deal. I sent him mine, he sent me his. Since I was young enough to be his son, believe me, I got much the better of this deal.

Several times yearly Ralph and I would meet and discuss our preaching. It was one great time, one super friendship. Plus it was like an ongoing postgraduate course in homiletics (the art of preaching).

One day in perusing one of my own books, I came on this phrase: "He daily spread his prayer carpet toward the First National Bank." Excellent writing. Superb phraseology. And where did I get it? I know. It came from my subconscious, inspired by my clever friend.

Many times in those journeys through my P.S. pages, I come on the signal "R.G.," meaning Ralph Gilbert. And many times in one of my notebooks I have seen this gem: "Regularly he made mecca to his stocks and bonds." (R.G.) Fine preaching, Ralph. Super. Anyone would get your point, and I did. Fact is, I got it so thoroughly it went way down in my interior. But when it came back, it looked like this: "He daily spread his prayer carpet toward the First National Bank."
Psychology may have an explanation for this. Psychiatrists also have their theories. So do the brain engineers.

But for me it sums up here—

   We are created with some mysterious hookup
to the Divine Mind.
  And if we develop
   techniques to help Him
    The Lord *will* express through us—
     something fresh
      something attractive
       something beautiful.

MY CLAIM FOR YOU

If you will devise your own technique, any usable technique for collecting picturesque speech, you will
   (a) never be bored
   (b) be more salable
   (c) have more fun writing

Assignment: For thirty days copy everything which deserves your label "Picturesque Speech." A statement you've heard, an item you've read, something you yourself said. Anything which might be labeled "fresh," "attractive," "beautiful," write it down.

Then at least every seven days for six weeks read these over. Muse, smile, ask the Lord to use them inside you. If after six weeks you've done this faithfully, I can tell you what comes next. Next you'll want another six weeks. Then six months, one year, two, and forever.

How do I know it will be like this? I know, because you've found one great new tool, one exciting way to grow.

And this too I know—you'll be a better writer!

58

TWO CAUTION NOTES:

1. Every sentence does not need to be different. Too much "fresh" can be ludicrous. I must not become a "twittering bird."

2. I must find for myself the fine line between originality and pilfering. Some places we must go single file, and personal integrity is one of those places.

13

Tools:
The "How-Not-Tos"

We learn more from positives than negatives. Certain
scholars of the mind assure us this is true. Positive experiences,
positive memories, positive input—all are positively important. Yet there is another school of thought which says the opposite, "We learn most from our trauma."

Principle: When so many brilliant minds come to so many
different conclusions, we do well to make up our own minds.

So the question is, "Where do I learn most?"

No doubt about it for me. I learn most from the positives,
but I also learn from the negatives. Because I do learn both
ways, early in my career I developed another technique. This I
call my "How-Not-To" collection. From printed books, from
newspaper and magazine, from anywhere I collect these "aw-
ful-awfuls." The way I use this material is to rewrite it and redo
it by my rules.

Assignment: Study the examples on the following pages
and rewrite. Using your own rules (or the six cardinal rules),
struggle till the meaning comes clear.

HOW-NOT-TOS

1. From a published book by a psychiatrist:
   "Her treatment of psychic creativity differs in several re-
   spects from those well-established approaches to the subjects to which psycho-analytic readers owe whatever famil-
   iarity with it they possess."

   _____

   _____

   _____

   _____

   _____

   _____

2. From a book on simplicity in spiritual living:
   "This perfect will of God, not despite its perfectness, but because of it, may so exceed our dust-clouded imagination,
   that we may fail to see that it is applicable at all, just as a
   small child may fail to appreciate disciplinary action which
   is designed for his well-being in later years."

   _____

   _____

   _____

   _____

3. Gross example of "how not to" from recently published
   book by a well-known minister:
   "But always I was there on Sunday—there in the pulpit looking down on the married woman and the not-so-trusted dea-
   con and the hundred others, and hurriedly repenting me and
   searching in my heart for some such words as might to them,
   in crisis borne by each small wind that chanced to blow,
   great comfort speak."

_____

_____

_____

_____

_____

4. Opening sentence of a book on biblical enlightenment:
   "North of the ancient city of Nineveh on the opposite bank of
   the Tigris River from present-day Mosul, and south of
   Mount Ararat, in the region of the Garden of Eden, in the
   long chain of the mountain fastness of Kurdistan, not far
   from the Turkish-Iranian border, lies the ancient town of
   MarBishoo and its historic and large cathedral."

_____

_____

_____

_____

_____

5. Nomination for most garish example? From an instruction
   paper distributed to dental students in one of America's lead-
   ing medical schools:
   "When the student begins his clinical training and is assigned
   a patient diagnosis and treatment planning is always carried
   out on a comprehensive basis even though treatment in
   some instances might be done on the block system on a limited basis." (Here I must tell you—if I simply cannot understand what the writer is trying to say, I label it "Hopeless"
   and move on.)

64

_____

_____

_____

_____

6. From a famous medical writer:
   "If one has occasion to observe in a young adolescent about to
   be graduated from high school his struggles over a choice of
   college, and particularly, over his course of study in that college, one cannot but be grateful to those who have made
   some effort to put at his disposal a survey of the complicated
   activities of life in which he will soon be forced to partici-
   pate in some capacity or other."

Note: For many years I copied these ultranegatives and dropped them in my "How-Not-To" file. Then when the time was right, I would rework them until they made sense to me.

With the passage of time and from years of experience, I began a new technique. I taught myself to redo these negatives in my mind. Now it really became fun.

Today I can rephrase anyone's "how-not-to," including my own, in a flash. No question—this tool can become one significant teacher for me.

Promise: Any tool you develop to correct the mistakes of others, and your own, will

65

    (a) be a source of endless enjoyment

    (b) make you more salable

Tools:
14   The Filing System

"It is better not to file than to file and not find."

It's an ancient slogan, taken from the logo of a well-known office supply house. I have also seen something akin in ancient writing of certain mystics. Thank you, office supply house. Thank you, mystics. Accessibility is a must for clipping and saving.

My filing system, developed forty years ago, is the epitome. There is simply none superior, for me. Very important item, that—make yours superior, for you!

I file by subject. A few examples selected from my card file (3"x5") are shown on the next two pages.

You will note that cards 1 and 2 make reference to particular books. In my reading as I come to something worth remembering, I write directly on the page. Sometimes as I read, I make a slash mark at the beginning and the end of whatever I wish to file. This is copied on the 3"x5" card.

In my early years I did all this paper work myself. Later when I had a secretary, she did it. Today Martha—best secretary I ever had—checks each book I read and records my findings.

How do I use the card file?

(See card 1.) Suppose I am interested in some fresh material on *anger*. I go to my file, thumb through the "Anger" cards, and those words "six rules" turn on some distant light. Now I go to that section in my library where I will find Hansen's book, *Common-Sense Living*.

On page 100 of this book I will find "Anger" in my own

1.

```
Anger                              six rules
                                      ...


      "Constructive Use of Anger, Hatred, and Rage"

                  COMMON-SENSE LIVING,

                      Hansen

                      page 100
```

2.

```
Giving                             brings joy
                                      ...

                WHY WE ACT THAT WAY,

                  John Homer Miller

                      page 85
```

3.

Expectant mother   prayer for
                                        ...

              See Clippings Notebook

                        Mother, page 1-B

4.

Healing   in New Testament
                                     ...

          See Letter File: "Healing"

handwriting. "Anger" on the left hand side of the page is my subject word. To the right I've written "six rules." Under "six rules" I find three dots. Those three dots mean that this particular card will be alphabetically filed under "Anger." (You will understand that I may have many cards on "Anger." These three dots under each subhead help me keep order in a particular section.)

Word of advice: Before you decide on a particular filing method, do some extensive research. Office supply companies, libraries, catalogues have materials for your perusal.

Don't hurry. Experiment. You are developing a lifetime helper here. A system self-tailored is all-important. Time, money, and effort at the outset will be returned manyfold.

You will note that card 3 refers to my Clippings Notebook. I have several of these notebooks on my shelves. Big notebooks for articles, stories, newspaper clippings, poems, magazine articles, special items.

Card 4 reminds me that this particular item is in my Letter File. Here I will find what I'm looking for in a file envelope, this one marked "H."

THE MISCELLANEOUS DRAWER

Another valuable addition to my system is the Miscellaneous Drawer, filled with cards unfiled. Always in my reading there are things I'd like to keep, but where shall I put them? When the answer doesn't come, these are typed on a card and placed in my Miscellaneous Drawer.

How do I use this drawer? Occasionally I thumb through it. I smile. I think, "How nice." Here I have a vast storehouse, a rich mine of priceless recall.

Note: Many years ago I put my card file on microfilm. Today I preserve it by computer.

THE ILLUSTRATIONS NOTEBOOK

Another adjunct to my filing system is the Illustrations Note-book. Here are stories from my own experience, stories I've used, stories I've never used, stories long forgotten. Most of us have happenings so loaded with drama, we think, "This I will never forget." But we do. So take it from one author who knows by experience—record your "unforgettables." One day you'll be glad you did. And especially you'll be glad when that editor says, "You illustrate so well. I'll buy!"

71

15 Looking Under the Hood—Self-Analysis

We have a new car. We call it our little red friend, and we love it. Who wouldn't? This particular little red friend gives us thirty-five miles per gallon around town. On long trips she purrs to the tune of forty purrs per.

Recently on a trip our little red friend was obviously hurting. We could hear it hurting, so we stopped for information.

"Where is the nearest dealer, please?"

"Nine miles off the freeway, east!"

Nobody likes to go nine miles left or right from the trip plan. Such a waste of time, but that's not all. In nine miles that strange sound takes on many options, and all of them awful.

Yet when we got there, the nice man said, "Let's look under the hood." There under the hood he found our problem. Taking his pliers, he tightened one small nut, and we were on our way. Is there any feeling quite like that?

"How much do we owe you?"

"For what? Have a good trip. Come see us again. Thanks for driving our car."

If only all our problems were that simple. A bolt loose here, a plug misfiring, that wire twisted, something trivial. But whatever the problem, small or large, the man's five words are worth remembering.

"Let's look under the hood."

I wish you could see my library of self-help books. So many

interesting titles here: *Our Inner Conflicts, The Art of Under-standing Yourself, A Few Buttons Missing, Listening with the Third Ear, Your Inner Child of the Past, The Transparent Self.* Fascinating stuff. Salable stuff.

But among these smiles and hairy dogs, if you looked long enough, you'd see another. This one you've probably never seen before. Somewhat bland and addressed to limited markets, it was a real nutcracker for me. And the title is: *On Not Being Able to Paint.*

I came on that title one day when I was rummaging in a library. Not being a painter, I almost passed it by. Then, as if by holy nudge, I was prompted to have a look.

As an example of writing, it is one grim book. Verbose, abstract. Poorly designed. Simply awful. Written by a psychiatrist who knew zero about communication. I am still glad he wrote it. If nobody else got his vague message, I did. And this is the message:

> "When diving and finding
>   No pearls in the sea,
>   Blame not the ocean
>   The fault is in thee."

That wasn't the doctor's poem. There was nothing that clear in his book. I can't think of a better way to summarize his thesis.

Thesis: If you've arrived at a time when your painting won't come, look inside the painter.

That same suggestion I need often for my writing. Very much I needed someone to tell me—

>   If I am to become a successful writer,
> If I am to create worthwhile material which sells and sells,
>   If I am to rise above rejection
>   and go on producing
>   I MUST DEVELOP THE ART OF SELF-ANALYSIS AS A
>   LIFETIME PILGRIMAGE TO A BETTER ME.

I am not a psychiatrist. I am not a professional psychologist either. As a pastoral counselor I have spent many hours listening to people's problems. I have attended the usual number of workshops, seminars, forums, assemblies in the general field of mental health. I also spent eight years on the board of a psychiatric hospital. I tell you these touches of my background to assure you once more that I know I don't know all I need to know.

But I do know this. Success in writing is first an inside job. I also know how exciting this thought can be. Why? Because once you've conquered the fear of starting, there is no trip to anywhere which can equal this—the trip to that inside you.

And if you'll be daring enough to take this trip, I promise you: You've discovered one more way to writing at your very best.

75

For me, looking under the hood goes on hour by hour, day by day, year by year. Certainly we can overanalyze. But those of us who are called to write had better discover some way to know how much is too much and how much is too little. How can we know?

Here too there must be almost as many answers as aspiring writers. You will develop your own unique testing places for personal progress from the inside out.

That's what I did, and I share with you now:

MY TEN SIGNS THAT I AM BECOMING A BETTER ME FOR BECOMING A BETTER WRITER.

-I-
I am becoming a better me for becoming a better writer if I am becoming increasingly honest about myself.

Questions: Am I growing in my ability to correct the places where I am wrong? Does the odd in me frighten me less? ,

Do criticism and rejection help me now because I bounce back quicker and grow with them?

-II-
I am becoming a better me for becoming a better writer if I am increasingly able to care about other people and their needs.

Am I unraveling my own feelings enough to focus on my reader's feelings?

-III-

I am becoming a better me for becoming a better writer if I am increasingly able to understand what's important.

Do I spend less time on trivia to concentrate more on the vital? Is the perfectionist in me doing right for right reasons?

-IV-

I am becoming a better me for becoming a better writer if I am increasingly able to organize my thoughts.

Can I adjust my vision to see the whole and how the parts fit in? Is there a growing rhythm and flow in my thoughts?

-V-

I am becoming a better me for becoming a better writer if I am increasingly able to use my subconscious.

While I am sleeping, relaxing, engaged in other things, are the subsurface workers producing in me?

-VI-

I am becoming a better me for becoming a better writer if I am increasingly able to concentrate on the positive.

Can I find new good in myself, in others, in the world around me?

-VII-

I am becoming a better me for becoming a better writer if I am increasingly able to wait.

Am I more patient with myself, with others, with the slow process of success in writing?

-VIII-

I am becoming a better me for becoming a better writer if I am increasingly able to think for myself.

Can I be independent when I should be? Do I follow the crowd less?

-IX-

I am becoming a better me for becoming a better writer if I am increasingly enthusiastic.

Are there fresh feelings of exuberance surfacing in me? Do I sometimes effervesce with what I'm doing?

-X-

I am becoming a better me for becoming a better writer if I am increasingly flexible.

Does the new frighten me, or give me zest? Am I conservative enough to value the old and liberal enough to keep an open mind? But not too open.

So this is the witness of one writer who has spent a lifetime in self-analysis.

77

> If I do believe that away at the center of me
> the Divine Creator has stamped His image,
> Then backtracking to the original has to be one
> of life's greatest thrills.
> There is no trip to anywhere as exciting as this.
> To discover what I was in the original
> To see me as I was intended
> To find the true Charlie again,
> This is pure joy.

Good luck! Have fun! And when you begin to tap the hidden lode of the hidden you, I can guarantee you, you'll be a better writer. I can also guarantee you'll be ready for two more big items.

SELF-ANALYSIS AND REJECTION

How many manuscripts with hope long gone are lying in desk drawers somewhere? There must be millions. And why are they there? One answer: rejection.

> On the arid plains of "somebody doesn't like me"
> bleach the bones of countless would-bes
> who never learned to take the bitter turndowns.

Some of these turndowns were self-rejections. After putting their words on paper, the disappointed authors gave up. They took it on themselves to decide: "Nobody out there will ever accept *me*." Others were turned down once by a single publisher. That did it for them. (For my own rejection record see page 82.)

Is there any way to keep from being wiped out by rejections? I think so. For one thing we can tell ourselves that no editor is perfect. One of the most successful pieces I ever sold was a magazine article rejected twenty-nine times before acceptance. Would you believe? The magazine which bought that piece had rejected it the thirteenth time out. Why? Was the editor's toast burned that morning? Had someone called him on the carpet the day before? Was he getting even by rejecting me? If I could muster even a little sympathy for the editor, would this help me with rejection?

Another word of advice from a veteran:

Do not call your unpublished pieces "Rejections." Give them some such hopeful name as "Dreams in the Shaping" or "Best Sellers in the Wings." (Akin to "Gems for Later" in Chapter 10, "Reread! Rewrite! Rephrase! Redo!" But with one difference worth noting—"Gems for Later" were rejected by *me*.)

Some places we must all go single file and I suppose rejection is one of these. So we must work up our own techniques, our own mental maneuvers, to handle disappointment.* But if we mean to be successful writers, this is one absolute necessity. Actually if we do assume the right attitude, another fine thing happens. We can turn rejection of every kind to our own good.

78

---

*Writer's Digest has an entire book dedicated to coping with the writer's internal and external stresses. Title: *The Writer's Survival Guide*. Subtitle: *How to Cope with Rejection, Success, and 99 Other Hang-ups of the Writing Life*. Written by Jean Rosenbaum and Veryl Rosenbaum, this book deals with such themes as: Using Rejection as a Catalyst; Psychological Blocks Against Creativity; The Special Problems of Success.

SELF-ANALYSIS AND THE POSITIVE USE OF CRITICISM

What can we do in the shower of stones? The first obvious answer is that we must develop our own self-image to its maximum. I go back often to read *My Ten Signs That I Am Becoming a Better Me for Becoming a Better Writer*. Here, I think, is the answer of answers when the rocks begin to fall. Do I like myself? Do I know I'm gradually improving? Only if I do know this can criticism help even while it hurts.

There is one more thing I can do. I can laugh. Some criticism is for laughs. And I share with you now one of my all-time favorite laughers. This one came after publication of my book *The Stork is Dead*.

Sir:

I hate to think what is going to happen to you in the last days which are coming soon when we are all going to be judged at the judgment seat like the Scripture says. The government ought to protect us from people like you. But there is so much evil in Washington I don't suppose they will do anything. I don't want my daughter to know the awful things that go on today between all those juvenile delinquents. Don't you worry about my Elizabeth. When she gets married, I will tell her all about her organs and what she is in for, and that will be soon enough.

Yours truly**

**From Charlie W. Shedd, *The Stork is Dead*, 2d ed.

Questions & Answers— Things I Know from Experience

16

Questions, questions. Wherever aspiring authors gather, there will be dozens of questions, hundreds, thousands.

Some intelligent, some not so; some thought out, others right off the top of somebody's head; all waiting for an answer.

In the next few chapters I am answering questions from my sources: (a) writers' workshops, (b) correspondence, (c) personal consultation.

You already know there are many things I don't know. But, some things I do know well. These I am sharing in this chapter.

Chapter 17 is my "limited knowledge" query list.

In Chapter 18 I defer to my editor at Writer's Digest Books. On now to "Things I Know from Experience."

MAGAZINES AS A LAUNCHING PAD
How can I break into the magazine field, and is this a good way to start?

This is an excellent way to start, and I should know. That's how I started. I had been writing regularly for woodworking journals.

If you are not a woodworker, this needs explanation. Writing for woodworker journals is not really "writing" in its purest sense. It is, rather, scratching off a set of dimensions, explaining parts and how they are put together. Good experience for sure because clarity is an absolute must.

Have you ever asked yourself, "Do I care enough about my hobbies, my specialties to write them up for others?"

When I decided to branch out, I began reading *Writer's Digest*. This little jewel includes in every issue selections telling us what editors are looking for.

You'll find this section extremely helpful. Reading it, some subject is sure to step off the page and wave you down.

For me it was a real launching pad and I became an avid reader of *Writer's Digest*. In almost every issue I found some spark to light my fires.

Out of this stimulus I wrote. When I was satisfied that my writing had merit, I sent it along. I picked choice one, choice two, choice three among the magazines. Who would I favor with this piece? Then?

Then I waited and waited and waited. Whatever could the problem be? Didn't *Writer's Digest* say this editor was looking for me?

Hard truth, hard to face! Editors do not sit around looking for me. They're doers, these people, and one thing they do is to attach and send rejections. But another thing they do is make mistakes. That being the case, I decided to develop a system which would make me less dependent on all those unintelligent editors.

Instead of writing one article, I would write three. Three different subjects I would develop. Then I would send those three different top-notch pieces to three different magazines. Next? Next I would write three more and three more and three more. You get the sequence. Finally I had twelve Charlie pieces in the mail all at one time.

Didn't work? What do you think? During the period I was using this system I sold more than fifty magazine articles. Fifty? Yes, fifty. Fifty with pay.

What does all this have to do with rejection? What it has to do is that I was being rejected, but it wasn't getting me down. Why? Because most of these rejections I never saw till long after. The secret? Martha was mailing my twelve fine offerings. She was also receiving them back with rejections and mailing them out again.

How many rejections would you guess those fifty salable pieces averaged? Believe it, eleven! That is over five hundred rejection slips in toto. (For more on rejection and how to take it see Chapter 15, "Looking Under the Hood.")

Did you pick up on that one item—pages back? *Writer's Digest* is still publishing their market list with specific topics and where they might sell. Thank you, *Writer's Digest.*

I should also add a word of thanks to one nice old lady whose name I've forgotten. She ran a magazine stand in the town where I was living. When I told her I was an aspiring writer and would like to browse her racks, she said, "Be my guest." Every month I would visit her store. She even furnished me a chair. Here I would ponder, I would jot down the name of certain managing editors and go from there. (Can you imagine the thrill it was for me—and her—when I took her a copy of my first book?)

On the magazine theme comes another frequent question: **Is it all right to send my articles to more than one magazine at a time?**

No, unless you let them all know what you're doing. Even then I think it's inadvisable. I learned the hard way that two editors might both like the same piece. If they both buy it, you have a real problem. That actually happened to me. A new secretary did send one of my articles to two magazines at the same time. They both liked it. They both could have laid claim to it and given me a hard time. Legally I had sold the same piece of my property to two people. Fortunately after I explained my predicament, one let me off the hook.

I have gone to considerable length to describe my method for one reason—I think it would be worth your time to develop a method of your own. If you start with magazines and succeed, you will

(a) encourage yourself with every acceptance

(b) establish your name in the marketplace

(c) make yourself more attractive to the editors who buy books

WRITING FOR TEENS—THAN WHICH THERE IS NOTHING HARDER

How do I write for teenagers? I work with the high schoolers at our church, and we seem to get along great. Sometimes when I prepare lessons, I get the feeling I should be publishing these thoughts. Since you write for this group, I wonder if you can tell me how.

"These are they who come out of great tribulation."

Writing for the teen scene is an ominous challenge. Here we aim for minds almost totally preoccupied with teen music, teen friends, teen phone calls, teen groaning and moaning, teen dislike of parents, teen struggle for attention, and often utter teen confusion.

Advice for the would-be teen writer:

Point 1: Write where they're at! (Negative sentence. Positive statement.) Where they are "at" is many things you don't know much about. But they are also "at" certain theme gaps you could fill in. Example: sex and dating. (See page 44.)

Point 2: Work your way into the teen scene and listen. Listen to the language. Listen for themes.* Listen to the questions.

Point 3: The final secret: Don't talk down to this crowd. Never, ever. They've been threatened, scolded, preached at to the maximum. Finger-pointing of any kind comes through like a broken record. One of their first questions about you will be, "Is this our friend?"

---

*How to Know if You're Really in Love, Fairway, Kans.: Andrews & McMeel, 1978, came directly out of the very thing I'm recommending. Made up of ten tests for marriageable love, this book was selected for a special article in the *Reader's Digest*. Since that article appeared, I have been inundated with invitations to colleges, universities, singles groups, and military bases. Why? Because the young do want help, and they will listen if you get on their wavelength and stay with their themes. And if they know you're their friend.

Editor's Note: Dr. and Mrs. Shedd for several years conducted "The Christian Writer's Workshop" through a grant from Lily Endowment. Aspiring writers were brought together in regional meetings to discuss Christian writing for the secular market.

The Shedds are widely sought for writers' conferences, seminars, and workshops. This section addresses itself to questions most frequently asked at these events.

NEWSPAPER SYNDICATION
OR
ARE YOU SURE YOU'RE READY FOR THIS?

How do you start writing for newspapers? I see certain columns, some of them national syndications, and I think I might like that. Do you think I would?

Yes, you would, and no, you wouldn't. But you won't find out unless you try, so here's one way to start.

Write a half dozen columns on some specific theme. Aim them first at the editor. You must get his attention, so find out all you can about him. Study his likes and dislikes. That's important because he makes the decision. Then when you're ready, call him for an appointment and show him what you've done. Give him some reasons you'd like to write for his paper. Tell him why you think you can become an attractive columnist.

Important tip: He's more likely to give you the nod if your proposed article is short and snappy. And remember: The more specific the better.

If the answer is "Let's go," you're launched on two rugged disciplines. First, you must discipline yourself to no-fail production. Then you must also discipline yourself to grab that reader's attention pronto (as in quick as a flash). But that's not all. After that sharp beginning, you must get better fast. You must keep getting better with each paragraph and close with a smash ending. Then? Then you must continue to do this with *every* single article.

That kind of discipline is why I ask: Are you sure you're ready for this?

Syndication is much more involved, and now you are swimming with the sharks. I should know. I have written three different weekly syndications extending over a period of sixteen years.

"The Meat of the Coconut" was a general column on whatever I thought might interest my readers. "Strictly For Dads" was aimed at fathers only. "How To Stay In Love" was for husbands and wives.

Writing your national syndication will be like raising the curtain on a whole new world. Details, details on the business scene, and you might even need a lawyer. You'll also need a strong-back mailman because letters come like you wouldn't believe. Yes, it's exciting, but sometimes you'll think you've fallen into another terrible trap. You've got to produce and produce and produce, and it's an awful self-regulation.

If you've decided you really want this, here's what you do—again, write a series of super sharp columns. Aim these too at the editor and remember he's seeing hundreds of proposed columns every year. So make yours superior. Then send that superior work to one of the newspaper syndications. (Ask your local paper for address.)

If after thinking all this through you're still interested, here's another discouraging word—all the syndicators tell me they are buying very little these days. Newspaper printing costs are out of sight. The market also is glutted, and the green light flashes seldom.

I said at the outset newspaper syndication is like swimming with the sharks. I must say, though, some of the syndicators I've known have been very nice sharks.

RADIO—IN AND OUT IN SIXTY SECONDS

Do you know anything about radio? I hear these little short things on one of our stations. They sound like such an easy way to begin. Can you tell me how I can break into this?

Do I know anything about radio? A loud yes, as in twelve years of "yes." During eight of those twelve years I did a piece for KNUZ, one of the major stations in Houston, Texas. The label: "Sixty Second Devotional."

In and out in sixty seconds—one minute to catch the listener's attention—sixty seconds to express one thought, include a Bible verse, close with prayer. Super training, and the station manager said it was one of their most popular products. Why would a devotional be so popular? He said it was because radio listeners are like this—they will not use their energy to turn the dial if they know what they're hearing now will continue for only sixty seconds. "So," said he, "we have a chance to hook 'em. One day they dig one item. Zap, we've got a fan."

Amazing, isn't it? So amazing I recommend it as one sure

way to keep life interesting. Do get on some local radio station if you can.

At some points writing for radio and for newspaper are almost identical. Pick a single theme and stay with it. Know your subject. Be enthusiastic. Listen to the station. Tailor your topic to their needs.

If your voice is not right for radio work, maybe the station would air your material with one of their announcers.

Another possibility: Could you write book reviews sponsored by a local bookstore? Or are you an expert in the kitchen? Most stations tip heavy on the side of housewife listeners. Think. Think. Think. What you know may be exactly what people need. It might also be what the station calls "hot copy"!

87

All this might particularly be a real plus in the early stages of your career. It will keep you writing and force you to a rigorous self-discipline. It will also keep your name before the public and that's good. Love that "P.R.," as in "public relations makes you salable."

Radio syndication is something else. If you're really thinking about radio syndication, my advice is *don't!* I had four years of it, and the trade label for this is "a hairy dog." Major problem here: You have almost no way to collect your money. Are these guys (a) dishonest or (b) just plain sloppy when it comes to paying their bills? I prefer "b," but some of my seasoned agent friends say the real reason is "a."

For several years I did a ninety-second spot. Labeled "Marriage Talk," this one was syndicated. To illustrate the possibility that "a" (above) may be the answer, hear this: Although I haven't been doing "Marriage Talk" for five years now, both my agent and I occasionally hear it today in places near and far away. Meaning? Meaning the station using it is probably still selling it to a sponsor. They're making money on it, caring not at all who's entitled to some of those dollars. How would you grade these people by "a" or "b" above?

Questions & Answers—
Things I Know Something About, Being a Smorgasbord of Many Items

17

How can I get published?

Always, spoken or unspoken, this is another prime question. Awesome question. Awesome answer.

In graduate school one of our professors was somewhat of a wag. With every new class at test time he would include this gem: "Define the universe and give three examples." Whereupon with nervous smile we would move on to question two.

I wish I had some quick-fix answer to "How can I get published?" Unfortunately I don't.

Yet always from every hopeful writer comes the plaintive plea "Tell me, please tell me, how can I break into print?"

If I Can Write, You Can Write was written as one author's answer to that cry.

You still insist on a condensed answer? How's this for a try?

You pray and mean it—

Lord, today I commit myself to becoming one fine writer. Help me to develop every talent you've given me. And one day down in the future, may You and I together become one hundred percent irresistible to the publishers.

Amen*

BOOK ROYALTIES
What is the customary percentage to an author? Do I take what

---

*When you're talking with the Lord, it's okay to use more than fifteen words per sentence.

they offer, or is this negotiable? Also how big an advance can I expect?

Most publishers make offers on an escalating scale. For instance:

10% for the first 10,000 books sold

12½% for the next 5,000

15% for all above that

Generally there isn't much room for negotiation in royalty percentages. Where you can negotiate is the advance. When your books have become best sellers, then you will be able to attract even more advance money.

Most publishers will tell you the standard sliding royalty scale is an absolute must. Without it, they say, they won't have enough money to promote. Are they telling it like it is, or are they putting you on? Who knows? But whether they are or aren't, I'd still negotiate that advance to the limit. With a healthy advance up front, your publishers are more likely to promote your books to recover their money.

FINANCIAL INDEPENDENCE
How long should I expect it to be until I can be financially independent as a writer? I'd be in heaven if I could only resign my job and do nothing but write. I guess what I'm asking is how long did it take you and what would you advise?

One of my friends took me to lunch recently. For several years he has been making noises about a novel he is writing. (In his case I think "planning" is the more accurate word. Or should it be "dreaming"?) My friend has a fine position with a considerable career ahead.

This particular day he had a new idea. What would I think if he resigned his job to spend one hundred percent of his time writing? His wife had agreed she'd go to work. Then when royalties started coming in, she could return to being full-time wife and mother.

Since my friend had already decided on this giant mistake, what could I say? He wasn't dining me for advice. All he wanted from me was a green light, which was not forthcoming.

Instead I told him a sad story and true. Another friend of

mine did quit his job to write. His dream? To produce what he forever after referred to as *The Book*. His wife went to work, and would you care to guess how long she's been working? Fifteen years. I think you should also know three years ago she wearied of supporting him. Today they are no longer husband and wife.

What is the lesson from this tale of woe? *The lesson is unless you have a key to the mint . . . unless your rich aunt died and left you a bundle . . . unless you win the lottery . . . or unless some other unforeseen dollars fall into your lap . . . hang on to your job.*

AGENTS

Do I need an agent?

Certain specialized writing might do better with an agent. (Radio writing, television writing, writing for movies qualify for the term "specialized.")

Two ways to find an agent:

1. Ask some author who has one.
2. Select one at random from those who advertise.

Fact worth checking: Does the editor I'm hoping to impress prefer to work with an agent? Most like working directly with the author.

What could an agent do for you? Good agents are market specialists. They know publisher trends. They also know editor preferences. Agents might also keep you on your toes. Although I've never sold through an agent, I did correspond with several at the outset. They seemed to like my potential even though early on my writing was too amateurish.

During this period I needed all the help I could get. In many ways I needed help. I needed encouragement. Encouragement comes in many ways, including certain hard shoves in the right direction.

I will forever remember this one response from a particular agent. What I sent him this time was a hurry-up job on some piece he'd suggested. By return mail he fired back a postcard. Two-sentence critique under a huge black blob. The two sentences: "Please don't send me any more second-rate offerings like your latest. This blob represents the mark on my wall which comes from beating my head there when you send me your worst." That must have been thirty-five years ago. Yet the black blob is still very clear, still very black. Still asking its question: Am I doing my best?

What do I think of agents? I think if you need an agent, if you can find a good agent, an agent might be just the thing.

One more time—back full circle! I must aim to make my writing so outstanding editors can't resist with or without agent.

THE QUERY LETTER

Can we discuss "query" letters? Is it important to write the publisher before sending my manuscript? And if I do, should I enclose an outline and a sample of my writing?

Always this is a lead question in writers' workshops, and it's a good one. Here too a warning: You could fall flat on your face before you've taken step one. All of my editors tell me they prefer inquiry first. One of my publishers receives so many unsolicited manuscripts annually, last year they developed a new system. They return all unsolicited manuscripts unopened with note: "Send outline and description. From same we will advise." Note they do not even say, "*Please* send outline."

(Technicality: Publishers are not required to return manuscripts. Unless you're a published author they'd be glad to hear from, you'd better include postage.)

What can we learn from this tale of sorrow? One thing we must learn is the art of query letters.

For starters, rule one is: I should limit the query to a single page. Why? Two reasons:

1. This busy editor probably has no more than one sheet's worth of time right now for me.

2. This editor is only interested in authors who can put their message in a tight package.

One of my editors tells this story. He once received an eleven-page inquiry letter and mistook it for thc outline of a proposed book. When he discovered his mistake, how long do you think it took to turn thumbs down?

If I were an editor, I would want that one-page query letter to include:

(a) proposed theme and purpose

(b) something about the author—a personal item or two released to the project and the record of anything previously published

(c) a flash of why it might sell

Can you query more than one publisher at a time? Yes. How many? Many, many. But one more time don't (do not as in not ever) send the manuscript to more than one publisher. Wouldn't it be exciting if two publishers wanted your masterpiece? Exciting? Yes. Fun? No. But this I do wish for you—that you may become so marketable, publishers all over the place will clamor for you.

COPYRIGHTS
What about copyrighting? How do you do this? Isn't there a danger people will steal my ideas?

Not much danger. In forty years I've had only one item pilfered. This was a piece called "Ten Commandments for Giving." A church envelope company stole it from me. For years they put it on every box of envelopes they produced. I like to believe the typesetter accidentally dropped my name. A bit shabby for an ecclesiastical firm? I think so. Especially after I called it to their attention and they didn't even answer. Nor did they change their typeset.

Let's talk first about copyrights for magazines plus all items other than books.

On everything you submit in final draft, up in the right hand corner put "Copyright." Then add your name and the date. Some authors I know send a copy of their work to themselves by registered mail. I don't think this attempt at proof of writing is worth the time it takes.

You can see I am a trusting soul when it comes to copyrights. But if you're not, an attorney can help you copyright officially. Then you'll have legal protection. (Your attorney will also have some of your money.)

93

My advice is don't waste even a minute, or the cost of postage, worrying about copyrights. Instead give your time to producing high-class material. Skill yourself until even a sneak would say, "No way! I would never dare to steal anything so fine."

Since most of what I have said refers to magazine articles and miscellany, you may be wondering about copyrights and books. No problem. With all your books your publisher takes over the copyright details. And another happy! They pay their lawyers to make it right.

94
HELP FROM ANOTHER WRITER
Is it a good idea to send your manuscript to another writer? I mean a published author. Would they even look at my material?

No, it isn't a good idea. You wouldn't believe the number of manuscripts which come unsolicited to an author. Will they even be read? I usually look at the first two pages and apply the red pencil. Then I return them with my rules. What happens? Almost always stony silence. Why? Because, say it again, most prospective writers are looking for accolades, not advice.

Another friend of mine sends manuscripts back with this form note: "If I took time to read all the manuscripts coming to me, when would I have time to write my own?" If you received a note like that, you wouldn't like it, would you? Yet it could be kindness in disguise. Even if that author did go over your work, this really isn't what you need. Again, the person you must please first is that editor. If I were you, I'd save my postage and (a) improve your work until you get the feeling "This is as good as I can make it," and (b) when you get that feeling, send it to the publisher and see if they agree.

REWRITE SPECIALISTS
Are rewrite specialists on the level? I see their ads in magazines like *Writer's Digest,* so I assume they must be honest. One ad particularly appeals to me, but I'm wondering.

Keep wondering. They must do a land-office business because they advertise continually. Let's hope they help some people, but I do wonder. If they are skillful enough to help you write, why aren't they writing their own material?

My experience with these "let-me-help-you-do-it-right" people was a pure negative.

When I started writing, when rejection slips were piling high, I saw such an ad. Sounded so fine: "Want to sell your book? Did you know, all it may require is a professional rewrite?"

On and on the ad went with other catchy phrases. Plus "iffy" words ("iffy" as in "may" from his second sentence, "all it *may* require").

You can believe this was one big decision, but off to the bank I went for a five-hundred-dollar loan. That was the man's fee.

Who won? He did. I still have the two manuscripts, mine and his. And knowing what I know now, mine is vastly superior.

Thanks for nothing, rewriter! True, you did what you said you'd do. You rewrote, rearranged, made changes, took my money. The bank also took my money, month after month after month. Therefore, be it clearly understood, my two words of advice on hiring rewrite specialists: "Do not!"

To be absolutely candid I think I turned to the rewrite specialist because I was looking for a shortcut. Be it clearly understood here also—there are no shortcuts.

WRITING SCHOOLS AND CONFERENCES
I get the feeling you're not much for writing schools or conferences. Yet you conduct writing workshops. Will you clarify, and if you think they're okay, which ones do you prefer?

My claim "If I can write, you can write" does sound like a put-down to all "aids and abettors."

But I can assure you it was never meant to be that. Schools, conferences, seminars, workshops, educational institutions featuring courses in journalism—these all rate high with me. I'm for anything which will help anyone become a salable writer.

You can never learn too much. I can never learn too much. But a note of warning: We can become "retreat bums." Meaning: We can wander so much looking for help, we forget that in the last analysis real help is self-help.

YOUR READER'S EYE
What do you mean by "remember your reader's eye"?

One of my friends published a book which I know was good material, but it didn't sell. I was sorry, because it could have helped so many. Why didn't it sell? I think one reason was tiny print packed too tight on the page. For today's reader, sentences, paragraphs, whole sections need to be attractively arranged.

Among the good things television has done, this is one sure plus—it has oriented us to expect the best in eye appeal.

Skillful editors know how to arrange copy so it won't be forbidding to a prospective buyer. But some editors do not have a good "eye." You must be ready to raise a fuss if they cram your words together. Sentences, paragraphs, whole sections need to be attractively arranged. Don't hesitate to make suggestions.

And remember you can also help get your idea across if you make certain your manuscript is

(a) "open" as in plenty of room, not crowded
(b) well spaced with short paragraphs
(c) divided clearly with subject headings

VANITY PRESSES
Is it ever a good idea to pay a publisher for printing your manuscript? I have a friend who did this. Since I haven't been able to find anyone who will accept my manuscript, I'm wondering. What do you think?

Answer: Ad from local paper:
"A representative from our publishing house will be in
your area. If you have a manuscript you've dreamed
of publishing or just a book idea, let us hear from
you."

It's a common ad with variation. One variation I saw recently:
"My salesman will be at said hotel from 9:00 until
5:00 on May 15th. If your manuscript is accepted, we
can get it out by December. Think how you'll feel giving your own book for Christmas."

96

If you go for this, what do you have? A basement full of Christmas presents.

One more time: The secret is to write so well that you are irresistible to the commercial editor of a commercial press.

THE MARKETING PROSPECTUS
Now that the contract is in hand, what's next? Should I sign pronto and return "Priority Mail"?

No. This is the moment to respond, "Thanks for your offer, but I have a question: What else will you do for me? Meaning: 'Let's talk marketing prospectus.'"

Nomination for super high in any author's life: when the mail brings that letter, "We like your manuscript. See enclosed contract."

Nomination for aspiring writer's super low: One year has passed and the royalty statements clearly show (a) this book has not sold, (b) it is not selling, (c) it probably never will sell.

Why didn't it sell? Many reasons, but one is that the publisher did not promote. Why? Because from its first returns, they could see this book was not a big one. It has not sold, is not selling, never will sell enough to merit their big push.

All this is why you do well to insist on a marketing prospectus. What is a marketing prospectus?

A marketing prospectus spells out in advance what steps the publisher will take to promote your book.

Next question: If I insist on a prospectus, could it turn my publisher off? No. The very reverse is true. Everyone up there—editor, general manager, sales manager—gets your message: "This author is *no* amateur. We must now call our marketing department and discuss some dollars for this book."

HARDBACK AND PAPERBACK
Who decides whether a book is published in paperback or in hardback? Does an author have anything to say about this?

Almost always this is the publisher's decision. Most of my books have been published first in hardback. So when do they go paperback? When a hardback begins to taper off in sales, the publisher takes that second look. If it's slowing down, but not too much, paperback may pump it up again.

Some books are released simultaneously in hardback and paperback; some in paper only.

You can ask your publisher to spell these steps out, but I've never done that. Why? Because I know the publisher is as interested in sales as I am.

Royalties on paperbacks are lower, but sometimes the wider distribution of paperbacks makes up for lower royalties.

TOO MANY BOOKS
Is there any danger that I might publish too much, get too many books going at once?

98

Yes, depending on your fields and your subjects. You will recognize two parts to this answer.

1. You might be producing so much none of it is your best quality.

2. You might also confuse your buyer. Too many titles too fast may leave the potential purchaser frustrated.

For further thoughts on this see page 134.

DIFFERENT PUBLISHERS
I notice you go with several different publishers. Other writers I read seem to stay with one. What's the rationale behind this?

Some publishers reach a particular market, some another. That's why I vary my choices.

In addition I find that moving from one publisher to another keeps them all alert. Publishers with exclusive rights do tend to become lackadaisical.

Advice to a new author: Cross out that clause in your contract which gives the publisher an option on your next book. That option is only for them. You don't need it. If you're good enough to publish once, they'll be glad to have you again. Others will too, and when that happens, you've kept the advantage in your hands.

Note: Often publishers won't allow first-time authors to delete the option clause. If you find yourself in that situation, ask: (1) that the clause be confined to the same subject (theology, cooking, bird-watching, whatever) as the first book, (2) that it specify "equal or better terms."

READING THE FUTURE
Is there such a thing as reading the future when you pick your subjects?

Sharp question, because it is possible for an author to waste time on trendy subjects. With the long time gap between writing and publishing, some hot themes do tend to cool.

Example: During the initial wave of drug interest, I decided to write a book on why some teenagers don't use drugs. One of my publishers and I conducted a mail survey in contest form. It solicited entries from those who had deliberately made a decision to reject the mind benders. Fresh idea. Unique approach. Very salable at the moment. However, by the time this manuscript was ready, the market had been sated. Most readers were rejecting eveything on drugs so thoroughly that even a fresh approach seemed tiring.

How can an aspiring writer manage the fickle Yo-Yo of human interest? One way is to put major focus on subjects which will always be fresh: courtship, marriage, parenting, grandparenting, teenagers, diet. Subjects like these create their own markets. Each generation brings new prospects, new buyers, new people in need.

PUTTING IT ALL DOWN
One writer I know says when she writes, she puts down everything she can think of, every thought, every idea. Then she goes back and sorts it all out. Is this a good way to write?

For her, it could be good. For me, no. My style is to make it the best I can sentence by sentence, paragraph by paragraph. If I were you, I'd listen to every successful writer describe his own techniques. Then I'd develop my own techniques, and I would aim to improve my techniques forever.

GRAMMAR
How important are grammar and spelling? I can just see my English literature teacher wince at some of my writing. Yet so many things today seem to sound better if they're not so formal. What advice can you give me here?

Most editors would tell you that everyday vernacular is

99

much more salable these days than proper English. At the same time it's a good idea for you to know correct English. Except for garish mistakes, your editor will tell you what's acceptable in the marketplace and what isn't. In almost every family, or among friends, there is someone well schooled in grammar. Such a person can be an invaluable critic. If I were you, I'd cozy up to this person and let him help me. And if you're married to one such, cozy up and praise the Lord. Often.

DICTIONARIES

When I look at dictionaries in bookstores, they confuse me with their differences. Which one do you recommend?

No favorite. I think you're wise to have several different dictionaries on your shelves. I do. Some are more erudite, others tend to common vernacular. Different dictionaries, like different translations of the Bible, can be real friends. Each with special slant can bring new light, fresh thought, a different touch.

Thesaurus? Same thing. My favorite is Roget, but do try to budget for several. These too can add that all-important touch, "I never thought of it like this before."

HUMOR

Humor is my thing. Do you have any special advice for me?

Yes, develop your kind of humor to an art. The world needs to laugh. Most publishers will tell you they like authors who can touch even serious material with mirth.

My own rules for humor:

1. Keep it clean.
2. Make it kind.
3. Remember, Charlie, always the most effective humor is humor which makes you look a bit silly. (Have you ever studied the reasons why this is true? Fascinating.)

Writer's Digest has some excellent material on humor writing. You might enjoy *How to Write & Sell Your Sense of Humor* and *How to Hold Your Audience with Humor: A Guide to More Effective Speaking*, both by Gene Perret.

100

QUOTES
What is your advice on quotes? I notice some writers use many quotes, others almost none. Why?

My word of advice on quotes is "Don't." All my publishers say, "Your readers buy your books to know what *you* think. That's what we pay you for."

Like all writing rules, exceptions should be made. But still for me it's an excellent one-word advisory: *Don't.*

ILLUSTRATIONS
Do you have any secrets for us on the use of illustrations? And where do you get them?

101

One of my professors was fond of saying, "There are sermons in stones and books in the running brook."

I like those lines from an ancient poem. They tell me that everything in my world is waiting to help illustrate. People, places, things, happenings—they all provide material if I stay alert.

(For further thoughts on illustrations, see page 71.)

THE JOURNAL
Almost everyone says, "If you want to write, you simply must keep a journal." Any thoughts for us on this?

Yes. I'm big on journals. My Picturesque Speech Notebooks (see page 53), my filing system (see page 67), and my Illustrations Notebook (see page 71)—all these constitute my journal. So those advising you to keep a journal are one hundred percent right on. I'd listen to them tell how they do it, what they keep in it, how they use it. Then I'd devise my own journal and faithfully tend it. One day it will be worth all the thought and every minute you've given it.

PLAGIARISM
Will you give us your thoughts on plagiarism? I have read about a famous writer who is being sued for using somebody else's material. Since suing is so popular these days, isn't this another danger if we do get published?

The Bible tells us, "There is no new thing under the sun."

Any writer who doesn't believe that may be in for a surprise. I've had this experience and you will. One day you'll be awed at your own brilliance. Suddenly a new idea comes, and you're sure this is one hundred percent original. Big thrill. Then at some future date comes the great fall. You read your idea or hear it from another origin in almost your exact words.

What happened? Take your choice. Maybe you and somebody else think alike. Or perhaps you read the whole thing years ago, then completely forgot it. Lying dormant in your subconscious, it suddenly surfaced one day in your writing. Or (my preference) the Divine Author chose you to express His idea again.

102

In the final analysis you're the only one who knows these answers: Am I, or am I not, a thoroughly honest person? Do I want to be? Does the ancient commandment "Thou shalt not steal" mean what it should to me?

Is your answer a solid "Yes" to each of these questions? Then I'd put aside my paranoia and get on with it. I would develop whatever safeguards I need. I would work out a sound philosophy of using, quoting, crediting. Then I would pray:

> Lord, thank you for all your truth and all who ever expressed it. I would be one among them. Keep me both honest and fresh . . .
>
> Amen

READING

So many of your rules seem to be built on extensive reading. Your Picturesque Speech and How-Not-Tos must come from things you've read. What kind of reading helps you most? Also do you have some reading program you could share, and when do you do most of your reading?

You're right. My Picturesque Speech and How-Not-Tos do come from a solid reading background.

One of my goals when I finished school was to read no less than one book each week. No, I haven't always reached that goal, but I have averaged fifty-two per year.

I'm a slow reader. I have taken some rapid reading courses, but these are not for me. I have the kind of mind which likes to meander down side roads. I like to read at a pace where I can ponder and mark, reread and muse.

My reading program:
   (a) I read what interests me.
   (b) I read what I think I should read.
   (c) I read what Martha recommends from her reading.
   (d) I read whenever I have a few moments.
   (e) I read sometimes instead of turning on TV.

Balance is another important checkpoint for a total reading program. What do I mean by balance?

For an answer, here is one of my favorite dialogues. It's between an old professor and a young sophisticate. They are sitting together at a banquet. She leads off with reference to a book on the current best-seller list.

   "Have you read this book, professor?"
   "No."
   "You really should, you know. Everyone is talking about it. It's been out nine months."
   "Is that so? And have you read Ecclesiastes or the Song of Solomon?"
   "No, as a matter of fact, I must have missed them both. Tell me more."
   "Well, you really should acquaint yourself. They've been out four thousand years."

QUIT REVISING
Doesn't there come a time when you should quit revising, settle for what you've done and move on? When is that time, and how do you know?

Yes, there is a right time to stop polishing and move on. When? One answer is my little prayer, "Stop me when I'm finished." (See page 130.)

Two other clues for moving on:
1. When I can honestly say, "This is my best."
2. When I simply can't stand to look at it one more time.

MONUMENTAL QUESTION—QUESTION NUMBER ONE
How will I ever find time?

Almost always when would-be authors come together, this question surfaces first. Since it is of utmost importance, I have given it a chapter of its own (see Chapter 19).

Assignment: (Sure it's repeat but "repeat" is a repeated part of writing.)

Someday when you can really spend time, do this—Go back through all my answers to the questions in this chapter.

Then do this—Check every place I've broken my rules.

Then do this—For an exercise in "I can do it better than he can" rewrite what I have said.

Then do this—Thank God for your ability to improve on what you read.

Questions & Answers—Things I Know Little About, Wherein I Defer to My Editor

18

The wisest person I know (praise the Lord I'm married to her) says—

"When you have nothing to say, say nothing!"

Thank you, sage friend, I hear you. I present now several often-asked questions where I should say nothing. In writers' workshops, in personal conversations, by letter they keep coming on. So I know they're important, and they deserve an answer. That being true, I've asked my editor at Writer's Digest Books to take over here. Since Writer's Digest has material on every conceivable author question, we'll do it this way. In some cases I'll tell you what I know and my editor will add to that. Others will be answered only by the editor.

CONTRACTS

One of the most discussed topics in any author gathering is contracts. Because this subject is so involved, I have asked my editor to tell us what he thinks we need to know. I have also asked him to recommend Writer's Digest books which deal with this all-important theme in detail.

The cardinal rule of contracts is "don't sign it until you understand it." If you have an agent, he or she will be of great help in this area. If not, you might wish to consult an attorney experienced in these matters. For answers to specific contract questions, as well as general information on literary contracts, the following books should be helpful: *Law and the Writer* (edited by Kirk Polking and Leonard S. Meranus), *The Writer's Legal Guide,* by Tad Crawford, and *Beginning Writer's Answer Book* and *Writer's Encyclopedia* (both edited by Kirk Polking).

RESEARCH
Do you have any special advice on research?

Very little, but my editor can help us. And somebody must.

Today's knowledgeable readers will not sit still for careless reporting. Neither will they stand for contradiction, sloppy preparation, inaccurate statistics, overexaggeration. And one further personal thought—though research is hard work, one day if a writer develops the right attitude toward it, research becomes part of the fun.

There are a number of excellent books on research. Among them are *Finding Facts Fast,* by Alden Todd, *Knowing Where to Look: The Ultimate Guide to Research,* by Lois Horowitz, and *The Craft of Interviewing,* by John Brady. *Writer's Resource Guide* (edited by Bernadine Clark) lists and describes corporations, associations, government agencies, and other organizations that provide information for researchers.

TABOOS
I understand there are certain taboos the writer must avoid. Can you tell me what they are?

You're right. There are universal taboos, territorial taboos, and specific taboos for specific subjects. In my field there are taboos which would not be taboo in other fields. Since this is an involved subject, I recommend the following Writer's Digest books which provide material on taboos: *Writer's Encyclopedia* and *Beginning Writer's Answer Book* (both edited by Kirk Polking).

PLAYWRITING
Will you tell us what you know about writing drama?

This is an especially challenging form of writing, quite different in many ways from the other forms discussed in this book. Raymond Hull's *How to Write a Play* is an excellent introduction to the field.

TELEVISION SCRIPTWRITING
Somehow I feel an urge to do television scripts, film scripts, things like that. Any advice?

First you must learn the rules of the game. *The Complete Book of Scriptwriting*, by J. Michael Straczynski, is a good introduction to this fascinating world. *The TV Scriptwriter's Handbook*, by Alfred Brenner, explores various kinds of scripts for television, as well as the television business.

WRITING FOR CHILDREN
Have you written for children? They say it's a good way to begin. Is this true, and could you give us some guidelines?

It is a good place to begin if you truly want to write for the young folks. But if you think it is an *easy* way to begin, think again. Many of the same disciplines in writing for teenagers apply here. *The Children's Picture Book*, by Ellen E. M. Roberts, and *Writing for Children and Teenagers*, by Lee Wyndham, are both helpful books.

POETRY
I write poetry, but I can't seem to find a publisher. Can you help?

Judson Jerome lists poetry markets in his monthly column in *Writer's Digest* magazine. There is also a very helpful section on publishing poetry in his book entitled *On Being a Poet*.

MYSTERY AND SCIENCE FICTION
I've always had a yen for mystery writing, detective stuff, maybe even science fiction. Are these overcrowded fields, and would you advise a new writer to concentrate here?

These fields wax and wane in popularity. But even so, there is almost always a publisher for an exemplary novel no matter what genre it is in. Dean Koontz's *How to Write Best-Selling Fiction* will help you decide where you should concentrate.

Monumental Question— How Will I Ever
19 Find Time?

These we have always with us—"time" questions. Here are some exact quotes from my mail:

> How will I ever find time? . . . As I look at writing for a possible career, I'm almost overwhelmed with the hours it must take to finally become successful . . . You wouldn't believe all I have to do. I don't think there is anyone in the world busier than I am. Understand?

Do I understand? And have I got news for you! This goes on forever. Becoming a successful writer does not lead to peace in the valley, or peace at your house, or peace at the typewriter either. So the more successful you become, the more you will be asking, "How can I ever find time?"

Answer: You won't. I won't. They won't. Nobody, but nobody, ever *finds* time for writing. Time for writing has to be *made*.

How then do we make time? For me, making time is first a matter of attitude. To shape my own attitudes I developed what I call "Charlie's Affirmations." Since they've been such a big thing for me, I pass them along with this hope: May you be able to reshape your mind for the maximum use and the maximum pleasure of each moment God gives you.

CHARLIE'S AFFIRMATIONS FOR TIME CONTROL, TIME USE, AND THE ENJOYMENT OF TIME
-I-
I will quit complaining.

I will tell myself this until I believe it—I have every bit as much time as anyone. The Lord of all time was very fair. He has given me twenty-four hours per day, seven days per week, and on and on as long as I'm given to live. Therefore, from this moment on I will waste no time fussing about time.

This affirmation is taken directly from my book *Time for All Things* (Nashville: Abingdon Press, 1962). Written in a situation where I desperately needed it, *Time for All Things* twenty-two years later sells on and on.

When we were visiting one day, a bookstore manager friend of mine made the unusual statement. Holding *Time for All Things* in hand, he said (reverently), "This one is a real little darling." A bit much? Certainly! But when twenty-two years later one of your books is still selling and selling, you will thoroughly agree, "This one is a real little darling."

-II-
I will develop the art of plunging right in.

Sharpening pencils, setting the thermostat, making a phone call, dally, dally, dally—all this has to go. So I must school myself for the quick takeoff.

One technique I find helpful is the "half-sentence stop." It's a mental trick, but for me it works, and this is how I work it.

At the end of each day's writing, I deliberately quit in the middle of a sentence. Or I stop partway through a phrase, a paragraph, a section. Then as I begin the next day, I am not starting from scratch.

Helpful technique: the "sweeper look ahead." Here I take a quick glance at what's coming. This also is a mental maneuver. It closes out the day by making deposits in the subconscious. There below the surface the whole thing has a chance to shape itself unknown. Mysterious, yes, but a very nice mystery—the Lord who created us created at two levels.

112

-III-
I will force myself to concentrate on one thing at a time.
Tipping my hat to the whole picture, I zero in bit by bit.
I am reminded here of this saying from a famous preacher: "I never sit down to write my sermon that I don't think of the people I should be calling on. Yet I never go calling that I don't think of the sermon I should be writing on."

-IV-
I will not be taken in by the myth of solitude.
"I must have quiet" is only another alibi. That means I am to develop my own peace even in the noise and chaos.

113

The Stork is Dead was written at a cabin far out in West Texas. Awesome stillness all around except for somebody's pet duck. Quack, quack, quack every day, sometimes all day, looking for a handout. Thank you, duck. You taught me much.

Affirmation VII in *Time for All Things* reads, "I will make friends with Divine interruptions." Thesis: "Man's interruptions are God's opportunities." If I believe that, couldn't this also be true? Many times the interrupter actually is more important than the interrupted. Can I think of my telephone as the Lord's instrument? Can I hear the knock on my door as His knock? And the quack of a duck? Maybe, since all the birds are His doing too, this duck can teach me concentration in the quack, quack, quack.

-V-
I will ask the Lord to help me love work.
And I do need help! Some days I loathe work. Some days I feel like the funny man, "I like work. It fascinates me. I can sit and look at it for hours."

There is a lovely story about a writer who has hit it big now. They are having a party in his honor. The scene is the lounge at his old newspaper, and mid all the "oohing" and "aahing" a cub reporter makes this comment: "Isn't it simply fantastic the way X woke up to find himself famous? I should be so lucky!"

Whereupon the grizzled old veteran retorts, "Remember, pal, he who wakes up to find himself famous probably hasn't been sleeping."

Since work and writing do go together, always and forever:

> Lord, help me to love work—
> always and forever!

"A professional is a person who can do his best work when he doesn't feel like it."

Alistair Cooke

114

20   Steps for Writing a Book

Warning: This chapter may be a drag. On and on forever, and where does it end?

Answer: It doesn't. Every author, every successful writer
knows about drag. And one place where we feel the drag is looking down the future to completion of a book.

That's what this chapter is about. It's about completion;
successful completion. For me the end is so locked into the beginning; so much tied to the whole process; I decided to give
you one author's start-to-finish steps in one giant look.

I have never written a book which tripped merrily along
from beginning to end. Somewhere, someday comes the heavy
drag. But for me there is no exception to this. A book goes better,
proceeds better, sounds better if I follow certain definite rules.

MY STEPS FOR WRITING A BOOK

1. *Birth* of an idea . . . from one of my incubators I hear noises
   . . . something new is hatching . . . I prepare it a nest in
   my subconscious . . .

2. Checking with the *Source* . . . is this one from Higher Reference? . . . or are these noises from some crack in my id?
   . . . there is enough neurotic material on the market without my secondary contributions . . .

3. *Sharing* . . . I discuss the possibilities with a friend . . . with an editor . . . with a successful writer . . . with anyone whose judgment I respect . . . above all I value the thoughts of that person who has been praying for me . . .

4. *Brooding* . . . thinking long in this field . . . jotting notes . . . gathering stories . . . collecting examples . . . sorting thoughts . . .

5. *Research* . . . reading books, magazines, papers . . . especially marking references to stimulate new thought . . . I listen to lectures . . . I listen to people . . . I listen to life . . . again, I make notes . . .

6. *Gathering* . . . pulling together material from steps 4 and 5 . . . clipping, pasting, stapling, filing . . .

7. *Outlining* . . . studying the material . . . brooding again . . . testing . . . visualizing . . . trying for the total picture . . . pondering till something comes clear . . . shaping until it begins to "feel" right . . .

8. *Organizing* . . . sorting my materials into initial outline sections . . . I, II, III . . . A, B, C . . . 1, 2, 3 . . . a. b. c. . . . putting sheets together . . . arranging in order.

9. *FIRST DRAFT* . . . writing a synopsis for each section . . . the fuller I make it now, the easier at later date . . . I try not to strain . . . I take what flows and then move on . . .

10. *Submit to editor* . . . I ask my editor to scan draft one . . . say it one more time—all editors are busy, busy . . . so I prepare this copy for clarity . . .

11. *SECOND DRAFT* . . . (this does not wait for the editor's letter . . . that may take three months . . . or more) . . . so I reorder . . . eliminate repetition . . . I begin to "tighten" . . . "polish" . . . this I call my "foundation draft" . . .

118

12. *THIRD DRAFT*. . . probably done in sections . . . on days
    when I'm up to a challenge I tackle one of the toughies . . .
    on less virile days I may write what comes easiest . . . I
    continue to "tighten". . . "polish". . . and this may go on
    for days . . . for days I sit there slugging away until I have
    said all I can, the best I can . . .

13. *FOURTH DRAFT* . . . rereading, rewriting, rereading, re-
    writing . . . by sentences, by paragraphs, by chapters I redo
    . . . at this point I begin some "holding" patterns . . . I lay
    it aside for twenty-four hours . . . forty-eight? . . . several
    days . . . then I reread again . . .

119

14. *Jazzing it up!!!!!* now the fun begins . . . I go to my Pictur-
    esque Speech Notebook . . . I jot down sharp things for par-
    ticular sections . . . I'm becoming excited . . . sometimes
    I'm carried away . . . I shoo off the twittering birds . . .
    then when I calm myself, I return to the manuscript bearing
    my good stuff . . . I place live spirits among the dead . . . I
    spizz up the slow movers . . . I add spizazz where needed .
    . . then back for typing again . . .

15. *FIFTH DRAFT*. . . when all has been retyped, I read the en-
    tire manuscript . . . I bear down hard again on my rules . .
    . I get tough . . . now, this step complete, it's back for an-
    other typing . . . the final preparation . . .

16. *Submit to the publisher* . . . celebrate!

17. *SIXTH DRAFT* . . . rewrite for the editor . . . study his
    comments, his ideas . . . I agree and disagree . . . usually I
    agree . . . editors are paid to know more than I know (about
    some things) . . . and especially I like it if I think they
    know more than I know about what will produce royalties
    . . .

18. *Now send it off with the prayer of release* (see "My Little Prayers," Chapter 22) (whether draft 6 requires retyping depends on number of changes) . . . I pray that it will (a) not need retyping, (b) sell a million, (c) be used of the Lord for His needs . . . (okay, okay, I know "b" and "c" should be reversed, and I'm working in that direction . . .)

19. *Meditation* . . . I take a period to unclutter my mind and tune in to the Infinite . . . this is a time of refreshing . . . purging . . . offering my mind for something new . . .

120　20. *I start my next book!* . . . This will be the best yet!

Note: There is considerable overlapping in all these steps. Some portions, sections, etc., do get more treatment than others. Some may even go through many more drafts than indicated here. I told you about "Kicks Have Kickbacks" from *The Stork is Dead*. What I did not tell you is that the book in its entirety went through sixteen drafts from beginning to end . . . You think that was a bit much? . . . Now hear this. The final chapter of *The Stork is Dead* was rewritten 127 times!!! But I did tell you this—*The Stork* after fourteen years has just gone into a second edition. Same song, another verse of "Reread, Rewrite, Rephrase, Redo."*

---

*For the curious: *If I Can Write, You Can Write* went through 12 drafts in its entirety. Some sections matched those 127 drafts above referred to.

Question: How long does it take to write a book?

Answer: From six months to twenty-five years . . . or forty**
. . . some sections . . . some paragraphs . . . some sentences
come with a rush . . . others after a long grind . . . From records
kept for the purpose: The last chapter of my *Promise to Peter* (a
2½-page chapter) required seventy-five hours . . . and that
book too is in its second edition with a title change to make it
even more salable (*You Can Be a Great Parent*) . . . It too goes
on selling and selling . . . Oh those hours!

   Assignment: Someday when you have the energy, reread
"My Steps for Writing a Book." Then putting your own needs,
your own style, your own ingenuity to them, you list your
steps. Certainly you'll revise and revamp, and this too goes on
forever. But I can tell you for your own writing there is no feeling quite like this feeling—
   I do know where I'm going!

**Addenda on the forty years . . .
   The thirty books I've written probably averaged one year, two years in their
writing. But one unpublished manuscript in my files has been there forty years, still
unpublished. Forty years shaping in my mind. But it's shaping! One of these days!
   Coincident? I wrote one book in six months to get it ready "rush" for a particular event . . . Result? My poorest seller.
   I think there are too many variables for an absolute answer to the question
"How long does it take to write a book?" Too many individual variables. Variables
of inspiration. Time variables. Variables of work methods. But never, ever, absolutely never any variable here—good writing, salable writing, takes time, time, time.

Twelve Gates to the Holy City; or, Exactly
21 Where Do I Start?

"There are twelve gates to the Holy City." That's what the All-Time Best Seller says, and we can be glad for so many options.* You choose one way, I choose another, yet we are all heading for the same place . . . sales, sales, sales . . . streets of gold . . . happiness forever.

One of the most asked questions from aspiring writers is, "Exactly *how* do you write? Do you do it by hand or typewriter or some other way? *Where* do you start, and as you go along, how do you keep order?"

Among the authors I know there are four basic methods.

Pen (pencil)
Typewriter (sometimes word processor)
Cassette or tape recorder
Dictation to another person

I have used all these methods, but my favorite is talking it to Martha. Or shouldn't I say talking *with* Martha.

If you can find a friend, an honest friend, to share your writing, lucky, lucky you.* And if your married mate can be this friend, add a few more "luckies." (If this latter possibility ap-

---

*For explanation of * see end of chapter.

peals to you, I have a suggestion—begin by promising him/her half those forthcoming royalties.)

On some books Martha is my coauthor. With others it's "Charlie only" on the jacket. Certain publishers insist on single-author books; something to do with promotion, sales. But on everything I ever wrote Martha has been my helper, my critic, my friend.

After our children were grown, she went to night school for a study of "Stenoscript." Stenoscript is modern shorthand, and it's a wonder. Today Martha can write as fast as I talk. So I talk what I plan to put in a book. She writes it down, then we discuss it thoroughly.

124

"STIFLE" OR "STIMULATE"?

"But couldn't this dual writing stifle individuality?"

Maybe for some, but our experience is the opposite. For us the word is not "stifle," it's "stimulate." We think it brings out the best not only in our writing but in our total relationship.*

As I dictate, Martha writes, but because she knows my rules, she's mentally checking . . . asking, "Why do you break the rule here?" . . . or, "This is inconsistent. Remember what you said back there?" . . . or, "You're not coming through clear" . . . or, "You've said enough; don't oversay" . . . or (my favorite), "Charlie, that is absolutely beautiful. But what do you want me to *do* about it?"

You must sense at once this kind of help is priceless for many reasons. And one of its solid reasons is that sentiment of the wisdom writer:

> Two are better than one,
> because they have a good reward
> for their labor. (Ecclesiastes)

TIME ADVANTAGE

Another advantage of tandem writing is more efficient use of time. Anywhere we're together (the two of us alone) we can write. In the car, on an airplane, this may be the very moment for sharing a thought and shaping it together.*

What's the matter with writing by pencil, by pen? Nothing if that's for you. One pen-and-pencil author friend writes 2,500 words per day, 365 days each year. That's what he says, and he does produce.

This would never do for us. Our writing tends more to "write when we're inspired." "Write when we must."

For me the early morning hours are best. Martha is the opposite. We joke about our differences and wonder how we ever made it. Me? I can hardly wait to get up every day and tie right into it. Some days I think Martha doesn't even believe in God before 8:30 in the morning and two cups of coffee.*

So we're poles apart in time-sync, but very much together where it counts, and where it counts is communication.*

Some of my writing is done alone in my early morning hours. I scribble. I put down my thoughts, cross out, shape up, produce. Then when Martha is fully awake, we talk, talk, talk, tear up, throw away, redo.* When we agree it's right for now, she types it. Then she leaves it for my next-day morning redo. How many times do we repeat the process? Many, many, many,* and this goes on until we both feel, "This is good. Together we like it."

125

ORDER

How do we keep order? If you have ever put a book together, you've surely had this feeling: "Oh for a table large enough to spread it all out where I could see it full scope, page by page."*

We have no such table, but we do have a substitute.

We buy several dozen clear-plastic folders, 8½"x11".

They come by several names, but ask for "clear-plastic report folders." They're not cheap, but they'll be well worth every cent they cost you.

With these we sort out material by units, sections, chapters, sometimes even paragraphs. Seed thoughts, notes to Charlie and Martha, notes to the editor, notes to be developed, bibliography, picturesque speech, possibilities varied and sundry—all sorted in plastic covers.* These we spread out for the total picture.

How do we know what stage we're in, which draft we're on? We know by color, the paper color.* Yellow means this, green means that, blue identifies another stage.* Then finally it goes on white for the editor. (White for "pure," "good," "very nice.") Does that last parenthesis come across as somewhat high and lifted up? Not to worry. Our editor will bring us down with red marks, black marks, and "This you must do over—better."*

126

---

*The asterisks in this chapter indicate deliberately broken rules.
Rules for all the rules:
Every rule is to be broken when
(a) it reads better broken
(b) the meaning is clearer

Suggestion 1:
Since you never finish your schooling . . . even if you're growing weary—
Go back through this chapter and ask yourself:
(a) Why was a rule broken here?
(b) Could I rewrite to make it better?

Suggestion 2:
Select another chapter of *If I Can Write*, or take any other book you've read, and read it again for broken rules . . . The mood is "picky-picky" now. Then train yourself to do this with almost everything you read—including your own works.

From all your reading you can learn both *how to* and *how not to*.

My Little Prayers for Better Writing

Those of us who believe in Divine creation have a significant advantage. Especially if we believe in Divine creation on a personal level, we do. Why? Because with this belief, the honest question is: Does the aspiring writer I see in my mirror have something more in mind than self-expression?

When we set our writing against the theology of Holy assignment, important things begin to happen. Tuning to the heavenly wavelength, we sense limitless possibilities. Then too when the way is hard, we have a helper, a comforter in disappointment, a Holy organizer. And when we reach the astral regions of super sales, super accolades, this too is absolutely priceless: We have a stabilizer, a vertical, whereby we keep our balance in success.

So here without further comment are "My Little Prayers for Better Writing."

MY LITTLE PRAYERS FOR BETTER WRITING

1. Prayer For Right Purpose
"Lord, write through me!"
Matthew 6:33: "But seek first his kingdom and his righteousness, and all these things shall be yours as well."

2. Prayer For Inner Cleansing
"Teach me to be honest."
Psalm 139:24: "Search me, O God, and know my heart! Try me and know my thoughts! And see if there be any wicked way in me, and lead me in the way everlasting."

3. Prayer For Discipline
"Help me to love work."
Luke 9:23: "If any man would come after me, let him deny himself and take up his cross daily and follow me."

130

4. Prayer For Skill
"Make me a pro."
I Corinthians 12:31: "Covet earnestly the best gifts."

5. Prayer For Termination
"Stop me when I'm finished."
Psalm 141:3: "Set a watch O Lord before my mouth, keep the door of my lips."

6. Prayer Of Release
"Here, Lord, I give it to you."
Psalm 37:5: "Commit your way to the Lord; trust in him, and he will act."

7. Prayer Of Gratitude
"Thank you! Thank you! Thank you!"
Colossians 4:2: "Continue in prayer, and watch in the same with thanksgiving."

23   Safeguards of Success

"Lo, how the mighty have fallen."

Straight out of the Book, this verse deserves a retake. Have you ever wondered why a particular writer did one good book and no more? Maybe two books? Three?

I have wondered that and for my own good have done some research. These are my findings. First, there are those who had only one good book in them. They quit because they got their message across. That's all they intended. Their goal was accomplished. Nothing wrong with that. They did their job. Rate them positive.

On the opposite side there is some negative news in my findings. Very negative, and this is it: For every one of those in category 1 I have found many in category 2. And category 2 consists of those who faded away because they couldn't handle success.

This is the reason for Chapter 23—I feel an urgency to share three safeguards for success I've tried to keep constantly before me. Praise God, I am one author who knows firsthand that success is one super experience. Yet from experience too I also know that success can be ultradangerous. This is why if we were sitting together I would say, "Even if you don't like this kind of talk, please don't stop me. I need to hear it again."

SAFEGUARD 1

With each new success I will recommit myself to hard work. I will not let up on my discipline. I will keep checking for continual improvement.

Again from the Book, another warning: "Woe unto you when all men speak well of you." I hope you can speak well of yourself, at least often enough to keep your spirits up. I hope you know when you're at your best and what makes your writing good. But if you're like I am, all things self-congratulatory need checking and rechecking.

134   So here's another question as an aid at this point: "Am I writing too much, overproducing?" Unfortunately, once an author hits it big, his publishers can do him in. They urge him to write and write and write; and you know why. Off successful writers they make their living.

When my books *Letters to Karen* and *Letters to Philip* hit the million mark I learned what a temptation over-writing might be. One day an editor (good friend by now) phoned. Quote, word for word:

Editor: Charlie, it is very apparent to all of us here that we need another book from you for our next year's list. What have you got for us? [Very heady stuff. I hope one day you'll know by experience.]

Charlie: Thinking over my own list right now, I draw a blank. I don't think I have a book just right for you.

Editor: Oh come on, Charlie. How about a book on "My Grandmother's Letters to Me"? With your track record that'll sell like crazy.

Hard to believe? Garish illustration? Sure, it's hard to believe, and it is a garish illustration. But you can count on it. When you have written your best sellers, the "bitch goddess" success will use every wile to lure you on. And if you're like I am, a sad thing happens. You begin to think you are much more important than you are. (Sure you're important in the original. Always you're important in the Divine Plan.) Yet this too is a fact: It is not important that you produce until you overproduce.

One more piece of advice, then, from a veteran. Whenever we take our cues from the wrong source, the drama of success can get awfully messed up.

I have written thirty books (published or in contract), and this is a fact—had I listened to my publishers, there would have been sixty.

"Lord, fill my mouth
With worthwhile stuff
And stop me
When I've said enough."

135

(Prayer of an unknown preacher.
Thank you, padre, whoever you were.
What a word for writers too.)

SAFEGUARD 2

With each new success I will recommit myself to meeting the needs of other people.

Fact: The more we walk in the sunlight, the more we tend to forget those who walk in the shadows. Why? Is it because our heads go soft with our comforts? We have solved our problems. Let them solve theirs. If they had worked like we've worked; if they had developed their skills as we developed ours; wouldn't they be up here where we are?

No, this kind of thinking doesn't happen all at once. It comes on padded feet and whispers ever so softly: "You made it. Enjoy it. You are among the best. Enjoy the best."

When you become a best seller, I do hope you'll enjoy what you make. But I do hope too you'll remember this ominous fact—some of the nice people who made it to the top were no longer nice people when they got there. Any mind-set too heavy with "I, myself, and me" does not produce nice people. Which leads to safeguard 3.

SAFEGUARD 3

For heaven's sake (my own ongoing heaven and other people's too), with each new success I will continually recommit myself to my basic values.

This is no fresh news. You've seen it, heard it, read it. Some fine folks who made it big collapsed morally. They fell apart from the inside out.

When you have made it to the top, you will meet many people on the fast track. In the media, in your public appearances, moving around on cloud nine, it will happen. You'll be introduced to some real high flyers. Then if you write in the self-help field, there will be another happening. Certain of these "beautiful people" will even share their heavies with you.

No exception, they too are beautiful people in the original. But some of them can hardly stand themselves now. They like what's happened *to* them but not what's happened *in* them. Inside something is terribly wrong; something is gone and they know it.

Why? One sad answer is that success brings with it the temptation to congratulate ourselves. Next? Next we begin making our own rules. We make exceptions to old standards. We forsake our roots.

So what is the answer? The answer is this simple rule, so simple it's profound, and this is the rule:

The higher we go, the more time we must spend on our knees. Doing what? Referring all our success to the Source of our success. Praying for humility. Thanking the Lord He has brought us so far. Telling Him that we will accept every added success as a Sacred Trust from Him.

Here I better close this safeguard chapter. I might be tempted to preach, and you're perfectly capable of being your own preacher.

But before I do put my pen up, I think you'd like to know one thing more. It's a prayer Martha and I pray often because we need it.

Lord, thank you for every dream realized
and so many more happy surprises in the wings.
But Lord, with every success, help us to live
so that we may always like what we see in the
mirror!

Amen

137

We Can Never Outgive the Lord—On the Abundance Foundation and What Will You Do with All Those Royalties?

24

David runs a peanut combine. Nothing unusual about a boy named David running a peanut combine. Except in this case it *is* unusual, because David is a retarded high school student.

All their lives retarded children have been told, "You can't" . . . "You'll never be able to" . . . or "Here, let *me* do this."

But the Presbyterian church in Virginia has a special thing going for retarded high schoolers. At the little town of Zuni there is a three-hundred-acre farm called Presbyterian Training Center.

Seventy retarded children live at Zuni. Here they are taught to work, study to their capacity and train for independence. Girls learn to be domestic helpers, and boys, like David, are preparing themselves for jobs.

Presbyterian Training Center is supported in part by the synod of Virginia, by parents, friends. But much of the operating cost is borne by livestock. Black Angus cows, bees to produce honey, a sizable chicken project, riding horses, pigs, and all of these have been provided by the Abundance Foundation.

The Abundance Foundation is a nonprofit tax-exempt enterprise supported entirely by 50 percent of the royalties from the Charlie-Martha Shedd books. Newspaper, radio syndication, cassettes add to the income. So do the numerous speaking engagements which come in the wake of writing success.

The purpose of the Abundance Foundation is hunger relief, and most of its grants are for animals. Dairy herds in Africa, water buffalo and goats in the Philippines, mules in Thailand, rabbits in Nigeria and Korea. In Ghana, Gambia, and India, chicken projects are at work. An extensive pig program has also been launched in Haiti, where poverty is a major problem.

The spirit behind all Abundance Foundation gifts has been summarized by one of our mission workers, "Give a man a meal and he thanks you. But though you have fed him, you have humiliated him. Give him the means to support himself, and you have given him the greatest gift of all—dignity."

After *Letters to Karen* was published in 1965, it quickly became a financial success. (More than two million copies in print, including foreign editions.) Followed by *Letters to Philip* (another million seller), *The Stork is Dead, Then God Created Grandparents, Talk To Me, Celebration in the Bedroom, Devotions for Dieters*, plus more and more best sellers, the truth came clear:

YOU CAN NEVER OUTGIVE GOD

So when the money questions come our way, this is the Charlie and Martha "never-you-doubt-it-even-a-minute-no-fail answer"—

If you want to be a successful writer, start this very day with a Covenant. Promise the Lord some definite percent of your writing income and never swerve from that commitment.

Fact: If you give in order to get,
you're a phony,
and God knows a phony every time.
Yet if you give in order to bless,
doesn't the Lord know that too?
He certainly does, and now He has
something to work with.

Why do so many buyers buy Charlie-Martha books? Martha and I like to think one answer is that they're good books; that they feed minds and lift spirits.

But this too we believe—
There are so many hungry in the world
 So many needy
   The Lord Himself guides buyers to buy
   To feed hungry bodies too.

Repeat:
  If you want to be a successful writer, start this very day
with a Covenant. Promise the
Lord some definite percent of
your writing income and never
swerve from that commitment.

141

25 The Ultimate Reward and the Inner Tribunal

They waited until everyone had left the hall. It had been a Valentine banquet, full house. This had been one of those nights when everything clicked, but I was frazzled. The adrenaline was running low.

Over at the side a young couple waited. I must admit that as I shook hands with the long line, my guard was up. Counseling now? Lord, help me find some hidden reserves, or maybe a side door.

But they weren't there for counseling. Reaching to take both my hands in theirs, they said, "We simply had to tell you what you've done for us. We were married six years—six awful years. Three children, and that was awful too. So finally we called it quits, got a divorce.

"Then someone gave us two of your marriage books, and we could never tell you the difference they made, how they opened our eyes. Suddenly we could see things we'd never seen before—mistakes we could correct and new possibilities. That's why we decided to start over.

"So here we are married again, and most of the time it isn't half bad, really. We thought you'd like to know about us. We also thought you might like to know that every night before we go to sleep, we read a chapter of one of your books together. Then we talk and share our feelings.

"We both agree now, the trouble before was our failure to communicate. And one reason for that was we needed something to get us started. That's probably the main thing your books have done, they got us talking. We just wanted to say thanks."

Then they turned and went off, hand in hand.*

For the writer who writes with Higher Reference, this is reward number one and this is the Inner Tribunal.

All we have ever said,
all we could ever say
comes down to this final question,
Who really is writing what I write?
Am I or am I not
an instrument
in the hand of the Divine?

144

*Charlie W. Shedd, "The Rewards of Christian Writing," in *Writing to Inspire* (Cincinnati: Writer's Digest Books, 1982), 295.

26 The Writer's Benediction

*May the Author of Words at their
very best and every good idea
Bless you beyond your wildest
dreams. And on that great day
when royalties clog your mailbox,
May He remind you how you did it
and what you can do to
keep this good thing going for Him.*

INDEX